A Disciple's Journal
Year A

Advent 2019, 2022, 2025, 2028

A Guide for Daily Prayer,
Bible Reading, and Discipleship

Steven W. Manskar
with Taylor Burton-Edwards
& Melanie C. Gordon

DISCIPLESHIP
RESOURCES

ISBN: 978-0-88177-914-1

Cover design by GoreStudio, Inc.
Interior by PerfecType, Nashville, TN

DR914

"O that we may all receive of Christ's fullness,
grace upon grace;
grace to pardon our sins, and subdue our iniquities;
to justify our persons and to sanctify our souls;
and to complete that holy change, that renewal of our hearts,
whereby we may be transformed
into that blessed image wherein thou didst create us."

→ John Wesley ←

Abraham + Sarah (Hagar → Ishmael)
                              daughter
                              ↓ Mahalat + Esau

Laban
  ↓ → unloved in-deceit)

Isaac + Rebecca

Jacob + Rachel + Leah   children
                (sister)   10

Twins: ① Esau ② ↓ Jacob (heir of
       (hunter)   (quiet) covenant)

Joseph + Benjamin

↓ Joseph

Jacob had 12 sons = 12 tribes
                        of Israel

Carol H6: 704-896-0844
Cell: 704-258-5045

Contents

Lent

Holy Week

Easter

The Season after Pentecost (Ordinary Time)

Articles

O that we could begin this day
in devout meditations,
in joy unspeakable,
and in blessing and praising thee,
who hast given us such good hope
and everlasting consolation.
Lift up our minds
above all these little things below,
which are apt to distract our thoughts;
and keep them above,
till our hearts are fully bent
to seek thee every day,
in the way wherein
Jesus hath gone before us,
though it should be with
the loss of all we here possess.

JOHN WESLEY
A Collection of Prayers for Families

How to Use *A Disciple's Journal*

John Wesley encouraged Christians to pray and read Scripture at the beginning and the end of every day. *A Disciple's Journal* is designed to help you habitually open your heart to grace by beginning and ending each day in the presence of the Triune God.

A Disciple's Journal contains two facing pages for each week of the year:

- **The left-hand page** includes the Revised Common Lectionary Daily Readings for each week.

  Sunday, the Lord's Day, is at the center. The lessons for Thursday, Friday, and Saturday prepare you for Sunday. The lessons for Monday, Tuesday, and Wednesday reflect upon Sunday.

  Lessons from the Old and New Testament are selected for each day of the week. The New Testament lessons for Saturday and Wednesday are from one of the Gospels.

  The lectionary includes two periods outside the seasons of Lent and Easter, Advent and Christmas called "Ordinary Time." The 33 or 34 Sundays that fall in the periods after the Baptism of the Lord and after Pentecost form a distinct sequence and are guided by the gospel of the year.

  The Sundays of Ordinary Time after Epiphany are designated by the number weeks after Epiphany, January 6. The length of this first Ordinary Time is determined by Ash Wednesday. Use the daily lectionary for Transfiguration Sunday for the week that includes Ash Wednesday.

  The Sundays of Ordinary Time after Pentecost are designated "Sunday between [Month] [Date] and [Date] inclusive." For example: "Sunday between May 24 and 28 inclusive."

  The bottom half of the page is divided into four quadrants that correspond to the General Rule of Discipleship (see pages 176–77). Use this space to record your acts of compassion, justice, worship, and devotion during the week.

- **The right-hand page** contains portions of hymns by Charles Wesley and excerpts from the Works of John Wesley. You will also find a prayer for each week based upon the Sunday scripture lessons. These prayers are written by members of the Consultation on Common Texts (www.commontexts.org). They are used here by permission.

If you are in a Covenant Discipleship group (see pages 178–80) or another type of small group, bring *A Disciple's Journal* to your weekly meeting. It will help you remember what you have done during the week. You may also record prayer concerns.

The Daily Lectionary

A lectionary is a way of reading the Bible centered on the life and work of Jesus Christ which shapes the Church's calendar. It unites the global Church in prayer and worship. The daily lectionary used in *A Disciple's Journal* was developed by the Consultation on Common Texts (commontexts.org). It is used here by permission.

The Revised Common Lectionary (RCL) is organized as a three-year cycle. Each year emphasizes one of the Synoptic Gospels. Year A is shaped by the Gospel According to Matthew, with significant portions of the Gospel According to John included during Lent and Easter. Because the RCL is intended for use in Sunday worship, it necessarily neglects significant portions of the Bible. The daily lectionary fills in the gaps.

Four Scripture lessons are selected for Sunday; two lessons from the Old Testament and two lessons from the New Testament. The first text is from the historical, wisdom, or prophetic books. The second is a Psalm that reflects a theme from the first lesson. The third lesson is from one of the epistles. And the final text is from one of the Gospels.

Prayer in the Morning and at Night

Pages 19 through 23 contain guides for daily prayer in the morning and at night. They are adapted from *The Book of Common Prayer*, which was the prayer book of John and Charles Wesley.

The collects for each day of the week are ancient prayers of the Church. Praying these simple guides of daily prayer with the collects is a way of joining your prayers with Christians around the world and throughout history.

The Psalm

Two psalms are appointed for most weeks. The first psalm is read with the lessons selected for Thursday, Friday, and Saturday. This psalm is also read, chanted, or sung in Sunday worship. The second psalm is read with the lessons assigned for Monday, Tuesday, and Wednesday.

Read the psalm to prepare your heart and mind before you read the other texts for the day. Reading the same psalm for several days helps you dwell in God's Word. Listen for what God is saying to you, the Church, and the world. Conclude the psalm by saying or singing the Doxology:

> **Glory to the Father, and to the Son, and to the Holy Spirit:**
> **as it was in the beginning, is now, and will be forever. Amen.**

The Hymn

A Charles Wesley hymn is provided each week. Hymns are an important resource for Christian formation in the Wesleyan tradition. Like the Psalms, the hymn for the week may be either said or sung each day. Take time to reflect upon the words and allow them to open your heart to God and his grace. Memorize the hymn along with the Psalms. The meter is provided to help you find a tune for singing each hymn.

A Cycle of Intercession

To help broaden your daily prayer "A Cycle of Intercession" is provided beginning on page 25. In the Lord's Prayer Jesus instructs us to pray "Your kingdom come, your will be done, on earth as in heaven." The cycle of intercessions encourages us to pray for the world each day.

A Blessing

I pray that *A Disciple's Journal* will be a blessing to you and your small group. If you are not in a small group for mutual accountability and support for growth in holiness of heart and life, I pray that you will find or form one.

> "Let us hold fast to the confession of our hope without wavering, for he who has promised is faithful. And let us consider how to provoke one another to love and good deeds, not neglecting to meet together, as is the habit of some, but encouraging one another, and all the more as you see the Day approaching" (Hebrews 10:23-25).

Rev. Steven W. Manskar, D. Min.
Pastor—Trinity United Methodist Church
Grand Rapids, Michigan
steven.manskar@gmail.com

Using *A Disciple's Journal* with Your Small Group

A Disciple's Journal is an excellent small group resource. The following are some examples of how the *Journal* may be used to help form disciples of Jesus Christ in small groups:

- Adopt the General Rule of Discipleship as your group's rule of life. Use the *Journal* to record how you have witnessed to Jesus Christ in the world and followed his teachings through acts of compassion, justice, worship, and devotion under the guidance of the Holy Spirit.
    - » The General Rule provides the agenda when the group meets.
    - » Begin with a prayer, read one of the Scripture lessons for the day, ask "What is God saying to us in this lesson today?"
    - » The leader then asks each person in turn, beginning with himself or herself, "How does your soul prosper?" The General Rule of Discipleship guides each person as they respond to the question.
    - » The group prays for each person after they've shared their response.
    - » The meeting concludes with singing a hymn, sharing prayer concerns, and praying the prayer for the week from *A Disciple's Journal.*
    - » Quarterly identify a specific area of the General Rule each person, or the group, wants to focus and grow; review the group's prayer concerns and goals.
- Advent, Lenten, and Easter study groups read the Scripture lessons for each day of the season and discuss the various themes, ideas, and images that emerge when they meet. Pray the prayer for each week along with the recommendations in the Cycle of Intercession.
- Groups may read and discuss the excerpts from *The Works of John Wesley* for each week.
- Read, reflect, and discuss the hymns of Charles Wesley. His poetry is a rich resource for study, theological reflection, and prayer.

Using *A Disciple's Journal* as a Family

Melanie C. Gordon

Ye that are truly kind parents, in the morning, in the evening, and all the day beside, press upon all your children, "to walk in love, as Christ also loved us, and gave himself for us;" to mind that one point, "God is love; and he that dwelleth in love, dwelleth in God, and God in him."
—John Wesley, *On the Education of Children*

John Wesley was committed to the education and formation of children. In his sermons, *On the Education of Children* and *On Family Religion*, Wesley emphasizes children's holiness and fitness for eternal joy with God; and the important role of parents in helping their children "walk in love". Praying together as a family is a tradition in Christian households. When we pray as a family, we connect with one another in a way that deepens intimacy with one another and with God. Whether we gather around the kitchen table, in the family room, or via technology when our families cannot be physically present with one another, daily prayer as a family offers the opportunity to grow in faith as children of God. The Gospels are clear that we are to make the way clear for children to discover Jesus. This is imperative in the church community, and in our homes where parents are the first and most significant teachers of their children. The home should be considered a sacred shelter, a place where "unconditional love, affirmation, challenges to accountability, and forgiveness are known; to learn and share rituals, symbols, and stories of faith; to recognize and claim their special gifts and mission in the world" (*Family the Forming Center*, Marjorie Thompson, p. 144).

As the world pulls parents in many directions, finding intentional time with our families can be challenging. Scripture tells us to teach children the words of God, "Recite them to your children. Talk about them when you are sitting around your house and when you are out and about, when you are lying down and when you are getting up" (Deuteronomy 6:7). Taking time to engage with one another and the world daily, strengthened by the love of God, is most effective when done in a pattern of time and rhythm. Family rituals create a sense of belonging, allowing each member to understand what is important in the family and offering a sense of identity. Rituals provide rhythm and consistency to our lives, allowing us to move spiritually from one place to another. Through ritual comes healing, connection and growth. What is realistic for a family that needs to get children up, dressed, fed, and off to school? What is realistic for families whose children are involved in activities after school, homework followed by dinner and bedtime? Each family has its own rhythm, and this guide is designed for families to create a rhythm in their life that intentionally includes time for family prayer, scripture and discipleship. Look at this as not just one more thing to put on an already hectic schedule. See this as a way to grow closer to God as a family, thereby helping children to engage in the world equipped as representatives of God in the world.

Setting the Space

Create a holy space or sacred space within the home. This can be as simple as a corner in the family room that contains symbols of faith—a candle, a cross, a small container of water, a cup, prayer beads, and a children's Bible. Take some time to ask your children what they think of when they think of God's love, and search the house for symbols that represent this.

Prayer boxes provide a concrete and safe place for children to share their prayers with God. Not all of us are comfortable praying aloud, and some children so not possess the language to share what is on their hearts. Writing or drawing their prayers offers children a way to release what they are feeling and hold on to these feelings while sharing them with God.

Prayer beads allow for a tangible way for children to relate to God. There are several ways to use prayer beads. Each bead can represent a prayer for a specific person or situation, beads can be held in the hand as a reminder of our connection with God, or beads can be used as the Israelites held fringe in their hands to remember that God will never abandon them.

Candles are a way to remind children that God is with us. Light a candle as you begin your daily prayers as a symbol that Christ is the light of the world. Encourage children to carefully blow out the candle at the end of your family prayers to symbolize taking the light out into the world as representatives of Christ in the world.

During Daily Prayers

Sharing scripture with children of different ages can be a challenge, and the Bible reading assigned for each day may be a bit overwhelming for children to sit through each day. Read the scripture ahead of time. Use a bible translation that children will connect with. After you read the scripture, simply share the narrative with your children in a way that you know they will understand.

Bless your children each day, as they are each a blessing from God who need to hear that on a regular basis. After daily prayers, take a moment and get on the physical level of each child, look each child in the eye, and with your thumb or pointing finger make the sign of the cross on their forehead and say, "you are a blessing." Children love being reminded that they are blessings in our lives.

Extending Daily Prayers

Three ways to use the Jerusalem cross as a visual reminder for children:

- **Make a copy** of the Jerusalem cross to place on the refrigerator or a central place in your home as a reminder for children of how we love God and offer God's love to others.
- **Let children draw a copy** of the Jerusalem cross, and then encourage them to draw or write how they have lived into works of piety and mercy each week.
- Since we live in a culture where we are often on-the-go, **keep a copy** of the Jerusalem cross in the car as a conversation starter for children to share how they have experienced acts of worship, justice, devotion, and compassion.

Taking the Light of God into the World

Serve the community as a family. Balancing our works of piety with works of mercy will allow us, and our children live into the command to love God and neighbor. Use the Jerusalem cross as a guide to help children find ways that you can serve others through acts of compassion and justice.

Children notice the world around them with awe and wonder, offering adults the opportunity to appreciate the world through their eyes if we only take the time to listen. Use time in the car, on the bus, or on the train to ask them what they noticed today that reminded them of something from morning prayer. They may need a little prompting, so ask them what they noticed during the day. You may also want to ask them what they wondered about today.

Guides for Family Prayer

PRAYER IN THE MORNING

Call to Prayer

The Call to Prayer in A Disciple's Journal *is quite appropriate for family daily prayer.*

Scripture

Choose one text to share from an age-appropriate translation of the Bible.

Silence

Keep the time for silent reflection appropriate for the ages of your children. As you practice as a family, the silence will become more focused and comfortable for the children.

Hymn

There are a couple of options for hymn singing. Recite or sing the hymn together, and ask the children which words stand out for them. You may also want to choose a hymn that they enjoy singing and make it a regular morning hymn.

Prayers for Ourselves and Others

Offer children the space to share their prayers. You may want to teach them the response, "Lord, hear our prayer" *following each prayer.*

The Lord's Prayer

The Collect

Use the list of Collects for Families appointed for each day. If your children are readers, and feel comfortable, allow them to take turns reading the Collects.

Blessing

Make the sign of the cross on each child's forehead and say, "As you go through your day, remember that you are a blessing" *or* "You are a blessing" *or* "Remember that you are a blessing."

Collects for Morning Prayer

SUNDAY

Almighty God, you are the source of all that is glorious. Fill our hearts with your gladness today, and in all we do today, help us worship you with gladness, through Jesus Christ and in the Holy Spirit. Amen.

MONDAY

All-knowing God, you offer great guidance for us each day. Open our hearts and minds that we will follow you joyfully through the challenges of the day, through Jesus Christ and in the Holy Spirit. Amen.

TUESDAY

God of peace, you sent Jesus as the Prince of Peace. Open our hearts that we will offer peace to people we encounter today, through Jesus Christ and in the Holy Spirit. Amen.

WEDNESDAY

God of grace, you offer us grace that we do not always deserve. As we encounter people today, help us to remember and extend grace to them, through Jesus Christ and in the Holy Spirit. Amen.

THURSDAY

Most Holy God, you are the greatest guide we will ever have in our lives. As we go about our day today, help us to remember that you will guide us through any challenges today, through Jesus Christ and in the Holy Spirit. Amen.

FRIDAY

Most Holy God, you created a world filled with mystery and wonder. In all we do today, help us to notice the beauty of this world, through Jesus Christ and in the Holy Spirit. Amen.

SATURDAY

Lord God, you gave us a world to care for and serve. As we go through this day, help us the notice and respond to ways we can serve you, through Jesus Christ and in the Holy Spirit. Amen.

PRAYER AT NIGHT

Call to Prayer

The Call to Prayer for Night Prayer in A Disciple's Journal *(page 22) is quite appropriate for family daily prayer.*

Scripture

Reread the scripture text that you and your family shared during morning prayer. Offer children an opportunity to share what they notice about the scripture reading.

Prayers for Ourselves and Others

Offer children the space to share their prayers. You may want to teach them the response, "Lord, hear our prayer" *following each prayer.*

The Lord's Prayer

The Collect

Lord, Jesus Christ, you made this day,
    and surrounded our work and play with your love all day.

Thank you for watching over us,
>   and bringing us together tonight as a family of God.
Bless and watch over us through the night. Amen.

Blessing

Make the sign of the cross on each child's forehead and say, "As you go to sleep tonight, remember that you are a blessing" *or* "You are a blessing" *or* "Remember that you are a blessing."

Collect for Evening

Lord, Jesus Christ, you made this day,
>   and surrounded our work and play with your love all day.
Thank you for watching over us,
>   and bringing us together tonight as a family of God.
Bless and watch over us through the night. Amen.

Find a list of Bibles and books for children at http://bit.ly/2o0gEjG

Family Prayer While Traveling

Our work and responsibilities outside of the home can take us away from our families for periods of time. **When you cannot be with your children**, adapt the daily prayers and Bible reading to share over the telephone or video technology to keep you connected to one another and God. To stay connected, let your children choose a symbol of faith that you can take with you on your trip. Plan a time for each morning and evening to connect. Use the Jerusalem Cross to share ways that each person offered compassion or addressed a social issue. This will open conversation about joys and sorrows of the day. Continue with a prayer followed by the Lord's Prayer, the Collect for Families, and a blessing for your child(ren).

When you travel as a family, let the children choose a symbol or symbols to carry with you. Plan a time for the family connect each morning and evening that you are away. Ideally, continue the same family ritual of daily prayers. If this is not possible, choose a space to gather as a family. Use the Jerusalem Cross to share ways that each person offered compassion or addressed a social issue. Begin with a prayer followed by the Lord's Prayer, the Collect for Families, and a blessing for your child(ren). This will continue the consistency and rhythm that children need to feel loved and secure.

Prayer in the Morning and at Night

A Cycle of Intercession

O for a heart to praise my God,
A heart from sin set free,
A heart that always feels thy blood
So freely shed for me.

CHARLES WESLEY
"O for a Heart to Praise My God" (1742)

Morning Prayer

CALL TO PRAYER (from Psalm 51)
> Open my lips, O Lord,
>> and my mouth shall proclaim your praise.
>
> Create in me a clean heart, O God,
>> and renew a right spirit within me.
>
> Glory to the Father, and to the Son, and to the Holy Spirit:
>> as it was in the beginning, is now, and will be forever. Amen.

SCRIPTURE   *The Psalm and one, or both, of the lessons for the day are read.*

SILENCE   *What captured your imagination?*
             What is God up to in this text for your mission today?

HYMN   *The hymn for the week may be said or sung;*
          the Apostles' Creed (see page 24) may be said.

PRAYERS FOR OURSELVES AND FOR OTHERS
> *See* A Cycle of Intercession *on pages 25–27.*

THE LORD'S PRAYER
> Our Father in heaven, hallowed be your Name,
>> your kingdom come,
>> your will be done, on earth as in heaven.
>
> Give us today our daily bread.
> Forgive us our sins
>> as we forgive those who sin against us.
>
> Save us from the time of trial,
>> and deliver us from evil.
>
> For the kingdom, the power,
>> and the glory are yours,
>> now and for ever. Amen.

THE PRAYERS   *The collect for the day of the week (see page 21) and/or the Prayer for the week is said.*

Collects for the Morning

SUNDAY

O God, you make us glad with the weekly remembrance of the glorious resurrection of your Son our Lord: Give us this day such blessing through our worship of you, that the week to come may be spent in your favor; through Jesus Christ our Lord. Amen.

MONDAY (*for Renewal of Life*)

O God, the King eternal, whose light divides the day from the night and turns the shadow of death into the morning: Drive far from us all wrong desires, incline our hearts to keep your law, and guide our feet into the way of peace; that, having done your will with cheerfulness during the day, we may, when night comes, rejoice to give you thanks; through Jesus Christ our Lord. Amen.

TUESDAY (*for Peace*)

O God, the author of peace and lover of concord, to know you is eternal life and to serve you is perfect freedom: Defend us, your humble servants, in all assaults of our enemies; that we, surely trusting in your defense, may not fear the power of any adversaries; through the might of Jesus Christ our Lord. Amen.

WEDNESDAY (*for Grace*)

Lord God, almighty and everlasting Father, you have brought us in safety to this new day: Preserve us with your mighty power, that we may not fall into sin, nor be overcome by adversity; and in all we do, direct us to the fulfilling of your purpose; through Jesus Christ our Lord. Amen.

THURSDAY (*for Guidance*)

Heavenly Father, in you we live and move and have our being: We humbly pray you so to guide and govern us by your Holy Spirit, that in all the cares and occupations of our life we may not forget you, but may remember that we are ever walking in your sight; through Jesus Christ our Lord. Amen.

FRIDAY

Almighty God, whose most dear Son went not up to joy but first he suffered pain, and entered not into glory before he was crucified: Mercifully grant that we, walking in the way of the cross, may find it none other than the way of life and peace; through Jesus Christ your Son our Lord. Amen.

SATURDAY

Almighty God, who after the creation of the world rested from all your works and sanctified a day of rest for all your creatures: Grant that we, putting away all earthly anxieties, may be duly prepared for the service of your sanctuary, and that our rest here upon earth may be a preparation for the eternal rest promised to your people in heaven; through Jesus Christ our Lord. Amen.

Night Prayer

CALL TO PRAYER

O gracious Light,
  pure brightness of the everliving Father in heaven,
O Jesus Christ, holy and blessed!
Now as we come to the setting of the sun,
  and our eyes behold the evening light,
  we sing your praises, O God: Father, Son, and Holy Spirit.
You are worthy at all times to be praised by happy voices,
  O Son of God, O Giver of life,
and to be glorified through all the worlds.

SCRIPTURE   *The Psalm and one, or both, of the lessons for the day may be read.*

PRAYERS FOR OURSELVES AND FOR OTHERS

Recall and examine your day. When did you meet Christ?
When did you deny Christ? When did you serve Christ?

THE LORD'S PRAYER

Our Father in heaven, hallowed be your Name,
  your kingdom come,
  your will be done, on earth as in heaven.
Give us today our daily bread.
Forgive us our sins
  as we forgive those who sin against us.
Save us from the time of trial,
  and deliver us from evil.
For the kingdom, the power,
  and the glory are yours,
  now and for ever. Amen.

THE COLLECT   *The collect for the day of the week (see page 23) and/or the Prayer for the week are said.*

Collects for the Night

SUNDAY

Lord God, whose Son our Savior Jesus Christ triumphed over the powers of death and prepared for us our place in the new Jerusalem: Grant that we, who have this day given thanks for his resurrection, may praise you in that City of which he is the light, and where he lives and reigns for ever and ever. Amen.

MONDAY

Most holy God, the source of all good desires, all right judgments, and all just works: Give to us, your servants, that peace which the world cannot give, so that our minds may be fixed on the doing of your will, and that we, being delivered from the fear of all enemies, may live in peace and quietness; through the mercies of Christ Jesus our Savior. Amen.

TUESDAY

Be our light in the darkness, O Lord, and in your great mercy defend us from all perils and dangers of this night; for the love of your Son, our Savior Jesus Christ. Amen.

WEDNESDAY

O God, the life of all who live, the light of the faithful, the strength of those who labor, and the repose of the dead: We thank you for the blessings of the day that is past, and humbly ask for your protection through the coming night. Bring us in safety to the morning hours; through him who died and rose again for us, your Son our Savior Jesus Christ. Amen.

THURSDAY

Lord Jesus, stay with us, for evening is at hand and the day is past; be our companion in the way, kindle our hearts, and awaken hope, that we may know you as you are revealed in Scripture and the breaking of bread. Grant this for the sake of your love. Amen.

FRIDAY

Lord Jesus Christ, by your death you took away the sting of death: Grant to us your servants so to follow in faith where you have led the way, that we may at length fall asleep peacefully in you and wake up in your likeness; for your tender mercies' sake. Amen.

SATURDAY

O God, the source of eternal light: Shed forth your unending day upon us who watch for you, that our lips may praise you, our lives may bless you, and our worship tomorrow give you glory; through Jesus Christ our Lord. Amen.

The Apostles' Creed

I believe in God, the Father almighty,
    creator of heaven and earth;
I believe in Jesus Christ his only Son our Lord;
    who was conceived by the power of the Holy Spirit,
    and born of the Virgin Mary,
    He suffered under Pontius Pilate,
        was crucified, died, and was buried.
    He descended to the dead.
    On the third day he rose again.
    He ascended into heaven,
        and is seated at the right hand of the Father.
    He will come again to judge the living and the dead.
I believe in the Holy Spirit,
    the holy catholic church,
    the communion of saints,
    the forgiveness of sins,
    the resurrection of the body,
    and the life everlasting. Amen.

Wesley Covenant Prayer

I am no longer my own, but thine.
Put me to what thou wilt, rank me with whom thou wilt.
Put me to doing, put me to suffering.
Let me be employed by thee or laid aside for thee,
    exalted for thee or brought low for thee.
Let me be full, let me be empty.
Let me have all things, let me have nothing.
I freely and heartily yield all things
    to thy pleasure and disposal.
And now, O glorious and blessed God,
    Father, Son, and Holy Spirit,
    thou art mine, and I am thine. So be it.
And the covenant which I have made on earth,
    let it be ratified in heaven. Amen.

A Cycle of Intercession

Prayers may include the following concerns if it is desired to pray for different topics through the week and the seasons.

Every day
- In the morning: the day and its tasks; the world and its needs; the Church and her life
- In the evening: peace; individuals and their needs

In Ordinary Time

Sunday
- The universal Church
- Bishops, annual conferences, central conferences and all who lead the Church
- The leaders of the nations
- The natural world and the resources of the earth
- All who are in any kind of need

Monday
- The media and the arts
- Farming and fishing
- Commerce and industry
- Those whose work is unfulfilling, stressful or fraught with danger
- All who are unemployed

Tuesday
- All who are sick in body, mind or spirit
- Those in the midst of famine or disaster
- Victims of abuse and violence, intolerance and prejudice
- Those who are bereaved
- All who work in the medical and healing professions

Wednesday
- The social services
- All who work in the criminal justice system
- Victims and perpetrators of crime
- The work of aid agencies throughout the world
- Those living in poverty or under oppression

Thursday

- Local government and community leaders
- All who provide local services
- Those who work with young or elderly people
- Schools, colleges, and universities
- Emergency and rescue organizations

Friday

- The president of the United States, members of Congress, and the armed forces
- Peace and justice in the world
- Those who work for reconciliation
- All whose lives are devastated by war and civil strife
- Prisoners, refugees, and homeless people

Saturday

- Our homes, families, friends, and all whom we love
- Those whose time is spent caring for others
- Those who are close to death
- Those who have lost hope
- The worship of the Church

In Seasonal Time

Advent

- The Church, that she may be ready for the coming of Christ
- The leaders of the Church
- The nations, that they may be subject to the rule of God
- Those who are working for justice in the world
- The broken, that they may find God's healing

Christmas

- The Church, especially in places of conflict
- The Holy Land, for peace with justice and reconciliation
- Refugees and asylum seekers
- Homeless people
- Families with young children

Epiphany

- The unity of the Church
- The peace of the world

- The revelation of Christ to those from whom his glory is hidden
- All who travel

Lent

- Those preparing for baptism and confirmation
- Those serving through leadership
- Those looking for forgiveness
- Those misled by the false gods of this present age
- All who are hungry

Holy Week

- The persecuted Church
- The oppressed peoples of the world
- All who are lonely
- All who are near to death
- All who are facing loss

Easter

- The people of God, that they may proclaim the risen Lord
- God's creation, that the peoples of the earth may meet their responsibility to care
- Those in despair and darkness, that they may find the hope and light of Christ
- Those in fear of death, that they may find faith through the resurrection
- Prisoners and captives

Ascension until Pentecost

- Those who wait on God, that they may find renewal
- The earth, for productivity and for fruitful harvests
- All who are struggling with broken relationships

All Saints until Advent

- The saints on earth, that they may live as citizens of heaven
- All people, that they may hear and believe the word of God
- All who fear the winter months
- All political leaders, that they may imitate the righteous rule of Christ
- All who grieve or wait with the dying

O that we might heartily surrender our wills to thine;
that we may unchangeably cleave unto it,
with the greatest and most entire affection to all thy commands.
O that there may abide for ever in us
such a strong and powerful sense of thy mighty love
towards us in Christ Jesus,
as may constrain us freely and willingly to please thee,
in the constant exercise of righteousness and mercy,
temperance and charity, meekness and patience,
truth and fidelity;
together with such an humble, contented, and peaceable spirit,
as may adorn the religion of our Lord and Master.
Yea, let it ever be the joy of our hearts to be righteous,
as thou art righteous;
to be merciful, as thou, our heavenly Father, art merciful;
to be holy, as thou who hast called us art holy,
to be endued with thy divine wisdom,
and to resemble thee in faithfulness and truth.
O that the example of our blessed Savior
may be always dear unto us,
that we may cheerfully follow him in every holy temper,
and delight to do thy will, O God.
Let these desires, which thou hast given us,
never die or languish in our hearts,
but be kept always alive, always in their vigor and force,
by the perpetual inspirations of the Holy Ghost.

JOHN WESLEY
A Collection of Prayers for Families

A Disciple's Journal
Year A

Help us to build each other up.
Our little stock improve;
Increase our faith, confirm our hope,
And perfect us in love.

CHARLES WESLEY

The Christian Year

The Christian Year organizes the worship of the Church to help Christians rehearse the life and ministry of Jesus and to disciple others in his way. The Christian Year combines evangelism, teaching, worship, the formation of disciples and mission, and helps the church keep all of these vital elements of its life and ministry constantly before it.

Advent

Orientation to Ultimate Salvation

The Christian Year begins with the end in mind. Advent is the season for orienting Christians to our place within God's work of salvation of the cosmos. Advent focuses primarily on the fulfillment of all things in Jesus Christ. It begins by reminding us of the second advent (coming) of Christ, the final judgment, the resurrection of the dead, and new creation. We then spend two weeks with the prophet known as John the Baptizer whose ministry and preaching about the judgment and end of this current age laid the groundwork for the teaching and ministry of Jesus. The final Sunday of Advent brings us to events leading up to the birth of Jesus.

Advent starts to work in us like a funnel. The purpose of a funnel is to concentrate everything that can flow into it into a smaller outlet so everything can fit into a smaller space. Advent takes in all of history from the "top" and concentrates it and all its meanings on one person, Jesus Christ. It takes in all time, past and future, and moving backward in time, leads us to the incarnation of God in Jesus Christ. It takes in whole cosmos and its complete renewal and leads us to the confusing and messy, which is to say, very human circumstances surrounding the birth of Jesus. It challenges us to take in the infinitely vast and incomprehensible and to see, hear and feel how all of it flows out of the son of Mary.

But the aim of Advent is not to fill up our heads with grand ideas. Advent, like the age to come it proclaims again and again, is intended to do nothing less that call us to repent and live the good news that God's kingdom, which will complete all that Advent describes, has drawn near.

This is why Advent was initially designed as a secondary season for preparing persons for baptism. Just as those preparing for baptism during Lent would be baptized at Easter, so those preparing for baptism during Advent would be baptized during Christmas Season, primarily on Epiphany.

As you read and pray daily this Advent, allow the funnel to do its orienting and re-orienting work in you. But more than this, expect the Spirit's refilling, even now, to make all things new in you.

Rev. Taylor Burton-Edwards

Dec 1 # First Sunday of Advent

Preparation for Sunday
Daily: Psalm 122

Thursday
28 Daniel 9:15-19
James 4:1-10

Friday
29 Genesis 6:1-10
Hebrews 11:1-7

30 **Saturday**
Genesis 6:11-22
Matthew 24:1-22

Sunday
Isaiah 2:1-5
Psalm 122
Romans 13:11-14
Matthew 24:36-44

Reflection on Sunday
Daily: Psalm 124

2 **Monday**
Genesis 8:1-19
Romans 6:1-11

3 **Tuesday**
Genesis 9:1-17
Hebrews 11:32-40

Wednesday
Isaiah 54:1-10
4 Matthew 24:23-35

The General Rule of Discipleship
*To witness to Jesus Christ in the world and to follow his teachings
through acts of compassion, justice, worship, and devotion under the guidance of the Holy Spirit.*

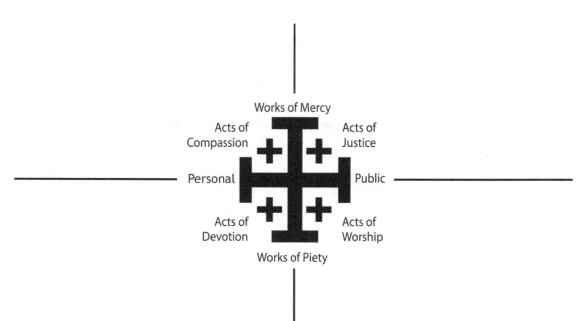

A Word from John Wesley

We see (and who does not?) the numberless follies and miseries of our fellow-creatures. We see, on every side, either men of no religion at all, or men of a lifeless, formal religion. We are grieved at the sight; and should greatly rejoice, if by any means we might convince some that there is a better religion to be attained, a religion worthy of God that gave it. And this we conceive to be no other than love; the love of God and of all mankind; the loving God with all our heart, and soul, and strength, as having first loved us, as the fountain of all the good we have received, and of all we ever hope to enjoy; and the loving every soul which God hath made, every man on earth, as our own soul.

"An Earnest Appeal to Men of Reason and Religion," 1744; ¶ 2

A Hymn from Charles Wesley

Hearken to the solemn voice,
The awful midnight cry!
Waiting souls, rejoice, rejoice,
And see the bridegroom nigh!
Lo! he comes to keep his word;
Light and joy his looks impart;
Go ye forth to meet your Lord,
And meet him in your heart.

Happy he whom Christ shall find
Watching to see him come;
Him the Judge of all mankind
Shall bear triumphant home;
Who can answer to his word?
Which of you dares meet his day?
'Rise, and come to Judgment'—Lord,
We rise, and come away.

(*Collection-1781*, #53:1& 5; 76.76.77.76)*

Prayers, Comments & Questions

Unexpected God, your advent alarms us. Wake us from drowsy worship, from the sleep that neglects love, and the sedative of misdirected frenzy. Awaken us now to your coming, and bend our angers into your peace. Amen.

*Hymns labeled *Collection—1781* are from *A Collection of Hymns for the use of The People Called Methodists* published by John Wesley in 1781.

Dec 8

Second Sunday of Advent

Preparation for Sunday
Daily: Psalm 72:1-7, 18-19

5 **Thursday**
Isaiah 4:2-6
Acts 1:12-17, 21-26

6 **Friday**
Isaiah 30:19-26
Acts 13:16-25

7 **Saturday**
Isaiah 40:1-11
John 1:19-28

Sunday
Isaiah 11:1-10
Psalm 72:1-7, 18-19
Romans 15:4-13
Matthew 3:1-12

Reflection on Sunday
Daily: Psalm 21

9 **Monday**
Isaiah 24:1-16a
1 Thessalonians 4:1-12

10 **Tuesday**
Isaiah 41:14-20
Romans 15:14-21

Wednesday
11 Genesis 15:1-18
Matthew 12:33-37

The General Rule of Discipleship
To witness to Jesus Christ in the world and to follow his teachings
through acts of compassion, justice, worship, and devotion under the guidance of the Holy Spirit.

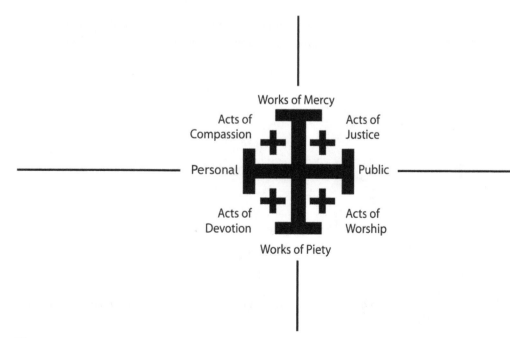

Works of Mercy

Acts of Compassion — Acts of Justice

Personal — Public

Acts of Devotion — Acts of Worship

Works of Piety

A Word from John Wesley

This love we believe to be the medicine of life, the never-failing remedy for all the evils of a disordered world, for all the miseries and vices of men. Wherever this is, there are virtue and happiness going hand in hand. There is humbleness of mind, gentleness, long-suffering, the whole image of God; and at the same time a peace that passeth all understanding, and joy unspeakable and full of glory.

"An Earnest Appeal to Men of Reason and Religion," 1744; ¶ 3

A Hymn from Charles Wesley

He comes! he comes! the Judge severe!
The seventh trumpet speaks him near;
His light'nings flash, his thunders roll;
How welcome to the faithful soul!

Descending on his azure throne,
He claims the kingdoms for his own;
The kingdoms all obey his word,
And hail him their triumphant Lord!

(*Collection-1781*, #55: 1 & 3; 88.88)

Prayers, Comments & Questions

Laboring God, with axe and winnowing fork you clear a holy space where hurt and destruction have no place, and a little child holds sway. Clear our lives of hatred and despair, sow seeds of joy and peace, that shoots of hope may spring forth and we may live in harmony with one another. Amen.

Dec 15

Third Sunday of Advent

Preparation for Sunday
Daily: Psalm 146:5-10

Thursday
12 Ruth 1:6-18
2 Peter 3:1-10

Friday
13 Ruth 4:13-17
2 Peter 3:11-18

Saturday
14 1 Samuel 2:1-8
Luke 3:1-18

Sunday
Isaiah 35:1-10
Psalm 146:5-10
James 5:7-10
Matthew 11:2-11 or
Luke 1:46b-55

Reflection on Sunday
Daily: Psalm 42

Monday
16 Isaiah 29:17-24
Acts 5:12-16

Tuesday
17 Ezekiel 47:1-12
Jude 17-25

Wednesday
18 Zechariah 8:1-17
Matthew 8:14-17, 28:34

The General Rule of Discipleship
To witness to Jesus Christ in the world and to follow his teachings
through acts of compassion, justice, worship, and devotion under the guidance of the Holy Spirit.

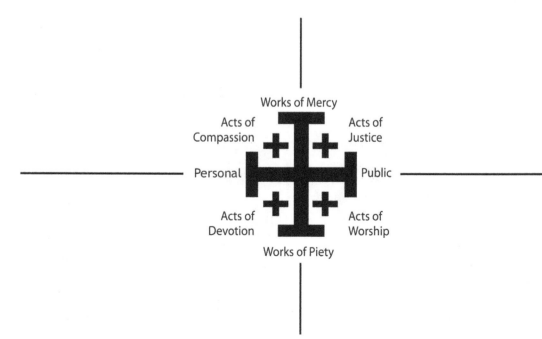

36

A Word from John Wesley

This religion we long to see established in the world, a religion of love, and joy, and peace, having its seat in the inmost soul, but ever showing itself by its fruits, continually springing forth, not only in all innocence, (for love worketh no ill to his neighbour,) but likewise in every kind of beneficence, spreading virtue and happiness all around it.

"An Earnest Appeal to Men of Reason and Religion," 1744; ¶ 4

A Hymn from Charles Wesley

Ye virgin souls arise,
With all the dead awake.
Unto salvation wise,
Oil in your vessels take:
Upstarting at the midnight cry,
Behold the heavenly bridegroom nigh.

Then let us wait to hear
The trumpet's welcome sound,
To see our Lord appear,
Watching let us be found;
When Jesus doth the heavens bow,
Be found—as, Lord, thou find'st us now!

(*Collection*-1781, #64:1 & 6; 66.66.88)

Prayers, Comments & Questions

O God of Isaiah and John the Baptist, through all such faithful ones you proclaim the unfolding of future joy and renewed life. Strengthen our hearts to believe your advent promise that one day we will walk in the holy way of Christ, where sorrow and sighing will be no more and the journey of God's people will be joy. Amen.

Dec 22

Fourth Sunday of Advent

Preparation for Sunday
Daily: Psalm 80:1-7, 17-19

19 **Thursday**
✓ 2 Samuel 7:1-17
Galatians 3:23-29

Friday
20 ✓ 2 Samuel 7:18-22
Galatians 4:1-7

Saturday
21 ✓ 2 Samuel 7:23-29
✓ John 3:31-36

Sunday *Ref. to Jesus birth*
✓ Isaiah 7:10-16 *8:23*
Psalm 80:1-7, 17-19
✓ Romans 1:1-7
✓ Matthew 1:18-25

Reflection on Sunday
Daily: 1 Samuel 2:1-10

23 **Monday** *gave promise for child Isaac*
✓ Genesis 17:15-22 *24*
✓ Galatians 4:8-20

24 **Tuesday** *26 Birth of Isaac*
Genesis 21:1-21
✓ Galatians 4:21—5:1

25 **Wednesday** *Joseph dreams + brothers jealous*
✓ Genesis 37:2-11 *50*
Matthew 1:1-17

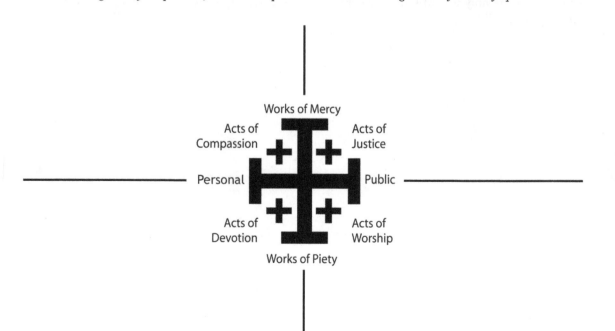

The General Rule of Discipleship
To witness to Jesus Christ in the world and to follow his teachings
through acts of compassion, justice, worship, and devotion under the guidance of the Holy Spirit.

Works of Mercy

Acts of Compassion — Acts of Justice

Personal — Public

Acts of Devotion — Acts of Worship

Works of Piety

A Word from John Wesley

Now faith (supposing the Scripture to be of God) is "the demonstrative evidence of things unseen," the supernatural evidence of things invisible, not perceivable by eyes of flesh, or by any of our natural senses or faculties. Faith is that divine evidence whereby the spiritual man discerneth God, and the things of God. It is with regard to the spiritual world, what sense is with regard to the natural. It is the spiritual sensation of every soul that is born of God.

"An Earnest Appeal to Men of Reason and Religion," 1744; ¶ 6

A Hymn from Charles Wesley

Father our hearts we lift,
Up to thy gracious throne,
And bless thee for the precious gift,
Of thine incarnate Son:
The gift unspeakable,
We thankfully receive,
And to the world thy goodness tell,
And to thy glory live.

Jesus the holy child,
Doth by his birth declare,
That God and man are reconciled,
And one in him we are:
Salvation through his name
To all mankind is given,
And loud his infant cries proclaim,
A peace 'twixt earth and heaven.

(*Hymns for the Nativity of Our Lord*-1745, #9:1 & 2; SMD)

Prayers, Comments & Questions

Shepherd of Israel, may Jesus, Emmanuel and son of Mary, be more than just a dream in our hearts. With the apostles, prophets, and saints, save us, restore us, and lead us in the way of grace and peace, that we may bear your promise into the world. Amen.

Christmas Season

The Aftermath of Incarnation

After Advent has "funneled" the cosmos into a Palestinian feed bin, Christmas Season opens up for us the global effects of the Word made flesh. Christmas Season is twelve days, starting with the Eve of Christmas, for the church to begin to unpack and wonder anew at all even the birth itself began to unleash then and continues to set loose now.

The readings for Christmas Season are full of violence, danger, and, bookended around these stories, blessing. We start and end the season (Christmas Eve and Epiphany) with the joyous announcement of angels to shepherds and Magi interpreting the stars. Between them we encounter the violence of Herod, hear of the genocidal deaths of thousands of male infants, and follow the family of Jesus on a desperate journey into Egypt not unlike the family of Jacob and their offspring had made. We remember the first Christian martyr, the deacon Stephen. We hear of Jesus' circumcision, and are reminded of the poverty of his family when we learn the sacrificial animals they could purchase for the rite of purification for Mary were those reserved for the poor.

All of these stories, and others we recount from the Bible, are there to keep us mindful that the kingdoms of this world do not welcome the coming of the kingdom of God, but violently resist it. They bear daily witness to the reading from John's gospel for Christmas Day. "He came to his own, and his own did not receive him." This is why we take the time to prepare persons and sponsors for baptism and discipleship. The world as we know it is not set up to receive our witness to Jesus. Indeed, it sets up myriad ways to put our witness to a violent and, from its angle at least, a shameful end.

But in and through all of these stories of opposition, we also remember the earlier words of our reading from Christmas Day. "The light shines in the darkness. And the darkness has not overcome it." And we are called to rehearse through these days, especially if we are accompanying candidates and sponsors toward baptism, that what we are given in Jesus is nothing less than to become, like him, children of God born not of our own striving, but by the will of God through water and the Holy Spirit.

Rev. Taylor Burton-Edwards

Days around Christmas Day

Preparation for Sunday
Daily: Luke 1:46b-55

December 22
Isaiah 33:17-22
Revelation 22:6-7, 18-20

December 23
2 Samuel 7:18, 23-29
Galatians 3:6-14

December 24 (morning)
Isaiah 60:1-6
Luke 1:67-80

Christmas Day
Isaiah 9:2-7
Psalm 96
Titus 2:11-14
Luke 2:1-20
or
Isaiah 52:7-10
Psalm 98
Hebrews 1:1-12
John 1:1-14

Reflection on Sunday
Daily: Psalm 148

December 26
Wisdom 4:7-15
Acts 7:59—8:8

December 27
Proverbs 8:22-31
1 John 5:1-12

December 28
Isaiah 49:13-23
Matthew 18:1-14

The General Rule of Discipleship
To witness to Jesus Christ in the world and to follow his teachings
through acts of compassion, justice, worship, and devotion under the guidance of the Holy Spirit.

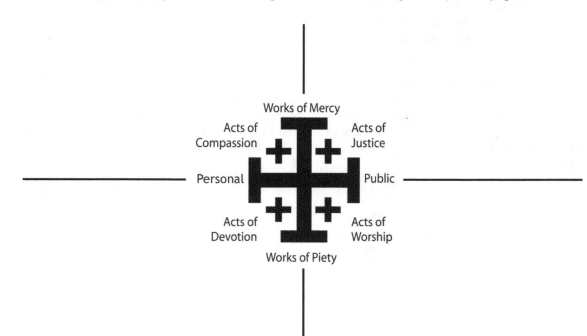

42

A Word from John Wesley

Faith, according to the scriptural account, is the eye of the new-born soul. Hereby every true believer in God "seeth him who is invisible." Hereby (in a more particular manner, since life and immortality have been brought to light by the gospel) he "seeth the light of the glory of God in the face of Jesus Christ;" and "beholdeth what manner of love it is which the Father hath bestowed upon us, that we," who are born of the Spirit, "should be called the sons of God."

"An Earnest Appeal to Men of Reason and Religion," 1744; ¶ 7

A Hymn from Charles Wesley

Glory be to God on high,
And Peace on Earth descend;
God comes down, He bows the Sky;
He shows himself our Friend!
God the invisible appears,
God the blest, the great I AM
Sojourns in this vale of tears,
And Jesus is his name.

See th' eternal Son of God
A mortal Son of Man,
Dwelling in an earthly clod
Whom heaven cannot contain!
Stand amazed ye heavens at this!
See the Lord of Earth and skies
Humbled to the dust he is,
And in a Manger lies!

(*Hymns for the Nativity of Our Lord*-1745, #4:1 & 3; 76.76.87.76)

Prayers, Comments & Questions

O Holy One, heavenly angels spoke to earthly shepherds and eternity entered time in the child of Bethlehem. Through the telling of the Christmas story, let our temporal lives be caught up in the eternal in that same child, that we might join shepherd and all the heavenly host in praising the coming of Jesus Christ, our Savior. Amen.

First & Second Sundays after Christmas Day
December 26–January 5

Daily: Psalm 20

Sun **December 29**
Jeremiah 31:15-22
✓ Luke 19:41-44

Mo **December 30**
✓ Isaiah 26:1-9
✓ 2 Corinthians 4:16-18

Tu **December 31**
✓ 1 Kings 3:5-14
✓ John 8:12-19

**First Sunday after Christmas
(Dec. 26-31)**
Isaiah 63:7-9
Psalm 148
Hebrews 2:10-18
Matthew 2:13-23

*The following readings are provided
for use when Epiphany (Jan. 6) is
celebrated on a weekday following the
2nd Sunday after Christmas Day.*

**Second Sunday after
Christmas (Jan. 2-5)**
Jeremiah 31:7-14
Psalm 147:12-20
Ephesians 1:3-14
John 1:1-18

Daily: Psalm 72

Wed
**January 1 –
Holy Name of Jesus**
Numbers 6:22-27
Psalm 8
Galatians 4:4-7 *or*
✓ Philippians 2:5-11
✓ Luke 2:15-21

Th **January 2**
✓ Genesis 12:1-7
✓ Hebrews 11:1-12

The General Rule of Discipleship
*To witness to Jesus Christ in the world and to follow his teachings
through acts of compassion, justice, worship, and devotion under the guidance of the Holy Spirit.*

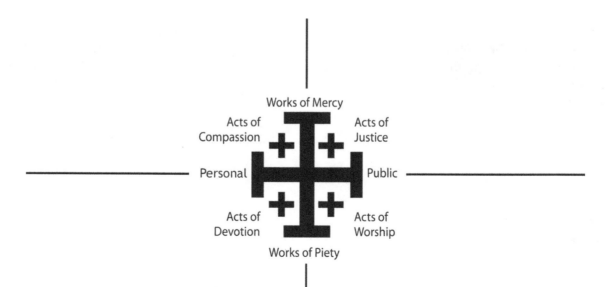

Works of Mercy

Acts of Compassion   Acts of Justice

Personal   Public

Acts of Devotion   Acts of Worship

Works of Piety

A Word from John Wesley

[Faith] is the ear of the soul, whereby a sinner "hears the voice of the Son of God, and lives;" even that voice which alone wakes the dead, "Son, thy sins are forgiven thee."

[Faith] is (if I may be allowed the expression) the palate of the soul; for hereby a believer "tastes the good word, and the powers of the world to come;" and "hereby he both tastes and sees that God is gracious," yea, "and merciful to him a sinner."

"An Earnest Appeal to Men of Reason and Religion," 1744; ¶ 7

A Hymn from Charles Wesley

All glory to God in the Sky,
And peace upon earth be restored!
O Jesus, exalted on high,
Appear, our omnipotent Lord!
Who meanly in Bethlehem born,
Didst stoop to redeem a lost race,
Once more to thy creatures return,
And reign in thy kingdom of grace.

When thou in our flesh dist appear
All nature acknowledged thy birth:
Arose the acceptable year,
And heaven was opened on earth;
Receive its Lord from above,
The world was united to bless,
The giver of concord and love,
The Prince and the Author of peace.

(*Hymns for the Nativity of Our Lord*-1745, #18: 1 & 2; LMD)

Prayers, Comments & Questions

Praise is our cry, O Holy One of Israel, for you have come among us and borne our burdens. Give us open hearts, that we might embrace our suffering sisters and brothers, and welcome Jesus in the hospitality we show to exiles. Amen.

Days around Epiphany

Readings through January 9 are provided for use if necessary. When the Epiphany of the Lord is transferred to the preceding Sunday, January 2–5, these dated readings may be used through the week that follows. When the Baptism of the Lord falls on January 11, 12, or 13, the corresponding preparation readings are used after January 9.

Daily: Psalm 72

January 3
Genesis 28:10-22
Hebrews 11:13-22

January 4
Exodus 3:1-5
Hebrews 11:23-31

January 5
Joshua 1:1-9
Hebrews 11:32—12:2

January 6
Epiphany of the Lord
Isaiah 60:1-6
Psalm 72:1-7, 10-14
Ephesians 3:1-12
Matthew 2:1-12

Daily: Psalm 72

January 7
1 Kings 10:1-13
Ephesians 3:14-21

January 8
1 Kings 10:14-25
Ephesians 4:7, 11-16

January 9
Micah 5:2-9
Luke 13:31-35

The General Rule of Discipleship
To witness to Jesus Christ in the world and to follow his teachings through acts of compassion, justice, worship, and devotion under the guidance of the Holy Spirit.

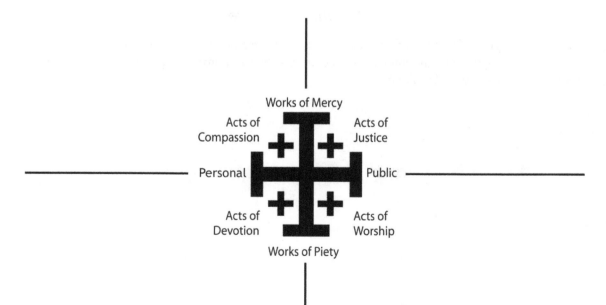

Works of Mercy

Acts of Compassion — Acts of Justice

Personal — Public

Acts of Devotion — Acts of Worship

Works of Piety

A Word from John Wesley

[Faith] is the feeling of the soul, whereby a believer perceives, through the "power of the Highest overshadowing him," both the existence and the presence of Him in whom "he lives, moves, and has his being;" and indeed the whole invisible world, the entire system of things eternal. And hereby, in particular, he feels "the love of God shed abroad in his heart."

"An Earnest Appeal to Men of Reason and Religion," 1744; ¶ 7

A Hymn from Charles Wesley

Where is the holy heaven-born child,
Heir of the everlasting throne,
Who heaven and earth hath reconciled,
And God and man rejoined in one?

Shall we of earthly Kings enquire,
To courts or palaces repair?
The nation's hope, the world's desire,
Alas! we cannot find him there.

Drawn by his grace we come from far,
And fix on heaven our wishful eyes,
That ray divine, that orient star
Directs us where the infant lies.

(*Hymns for the Nativity of Our Lord*-1745, #17: 1, 2, & 6; LM)

Prayers, Comments & Questions

O God of light and peace, whose glory, shining in the child of Bethlehem, still draws the nations to yourself: dispel the darkness that shrouds our path, that we may come to kneel before Christ in true worship, offer him our hearts and souls, and return from his presence to live as he has taught. Amen.

The Season after Epiphany (Ordinary Time)

The Season of Evangelism

The Season after Epiphany is bookended by two celebrations: Baptism of the Lord, on the first Sunday after Epiphany and The Transfiguration of Jesus on the last Sunday, prior to Ash Wednesday. The sweep of these Sundays and the days between them prefigures the sweep of the Christian life, from justification and initiation (Baptism of the Lord) to entire sanctification (Transfiguration). While this season is of varying length because of the varying dates of Easter, and so the varying starting time for Ash Wednesday, its purpose is always to help the congregation "get ready to get ready." That is, this is the "introductory course," if you will, to the more intensive preparation for baptism and new commitments in discipleship Lent is designed to help the church undertake.

On the Sundays between Baptism of the Lord and Transfiguration, the Sunday readings from the Old Testament are chosen to correspond with the gospel readings, which cover the early ministry of Jesus and in particular his calling of disciples. The Old Testament and gospel readings thus particularly support the evangelistic work of the church reaching out to others during these weeks. The Epistle readings are not chosen to correspond with the other two, but rather to present a "semi-continuous" reading that will be picked up again during the Season after Pentecost. Though the Epistle readings do not directly connect to the gospel, they do still lay out basics of Christian life. One might say that the Epistle readings are there to evangelize the church by helping the church "get its own act together" as it prepares to accompany persons in intensive formation in the way of Jesus during Lent.

This gives individuals reading daily and worship leaders planning for weekly celebration two distinct paths they may follow during this season, either of which may contribute to this season's evangelistic purpose. As you undertake your readings through these weeks, you may wish to coordinate the attention you give to the daily readings based on the focus your worship leaders have chosen for Lord's Day worship to gain the maximum benefit from the correlation of the two.

Rev. Taylor Burton-Edwards

First Sunday after the Epiphany
Baptism of the Lord

Preparation for Sunday
Daily: Psalm 29

Thursday
1 Samuel 3:1-9
Acts 9:1-9

Friday
1 Samuel 3:10—4:1a
Acts 9:10-19a

Saturday
1 Samuel 7:3-17
Acts 9:19b-31

Sunday
Isaiah 42:1-9
Psalm 29
Acts 10:34-43
Matthew 3:13-17

Reflection on Sunday
Daily: Psalm 89:5-37

Monday
Genesis 35:1-15
Acts 10:44-48

Tuesday
Jeremiah 1:4-10
Acts 8:4-13

Wednesday
Isaiah 51:1-16
Matthew 12:15-21

The General Rule of Discipleship
To witness to Jesus Christ in the world and to follow his teachings
through acts of compassion, justice, worship, and devotion under the guidance of the Holy Spirit.

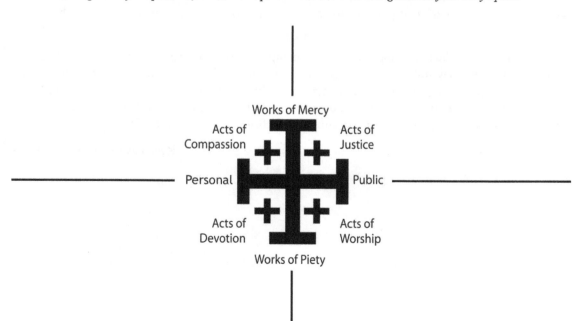

A Word from John Wesley

By this faith we are saved from all uneasiness of mind, from the anguish of a wounded spirit, from discontent, from fear and sorrow of heart, and from that inexpressible listlessness and weariness, both of the world and of ourselves, which we had so helplessly laboured under for many years; especially when we were out of the hurry of the world, and sunk into calm reflection. In this we find that love of God, and of all mankind, which we had elsewhere sought in vain. This we know and feel, and therefore cannot but declare, saves every one that partakes of it, both from sin and misery, from every unhappy and every unholy temper.

"An Earnest Appeal to Men of Reason and Religion," 1744; ¶ 8

A Hymn from Charles Wesley

Come, let us use the grace divine,
And all, with one accord,
In a perpetual covenant join
Ourselves to Christ the Lord.

Give up ourselves, through Jesu's power,
His name to glorify;
And promise, in this sacred hour,
For God to live and die.

The covenant we this moment make
Be ever kept in mind:
We will no more our God forsake,
Or cast his words behind.

To each the covenant blood apply,
Which takes our sins away;
And register our names on high,
And keep us to that day.

(*Short Hymns on Select Passages of Holy Scripture*-1762; CMD)

Prayers, Comments & Questions

Creator God, our soul's delight, your voice thunders over the waters, liberating the future from the past. In the Spirit's power and the waters of rebirth, Jesus was declared your blessed and beloved Son; may we recall our baptism and be disciples of the Anointed One. Amen.

Second Sunday after the Epiphany

Preparation for Sunday
Daily: Psalm 40:1-11

16 Thursday
Isaiah 22:15-25
Galatians 1:6-12

17 Friday
Genesis 27:30-38
Acts 1:1-5

18 Saturday
1 Kings 19:19-21
Luke 5:1-11

19 Sunday
Isaiah 49:1-7
Psalm 40:1-11
1 Corinthians 1:1-9
John 1:29-42

Reflection on Sunday
Daily: Psalm 40:6-17

20 Monday
Exodus 12:1-13, 21-28
Acts 8:26-40

21 Tuesday
Isaiah 53:1-12
Hebrews 10:1-4

23 Wednesday
Isaiah 48:12-21
Matthew 9:14-17

The General Rule of Discipleship
To witness to Jesus Christ in the world and to follow his teachings
through acts of compassion, justice, worship, and devotion under the guidance of the Holy Spirit.

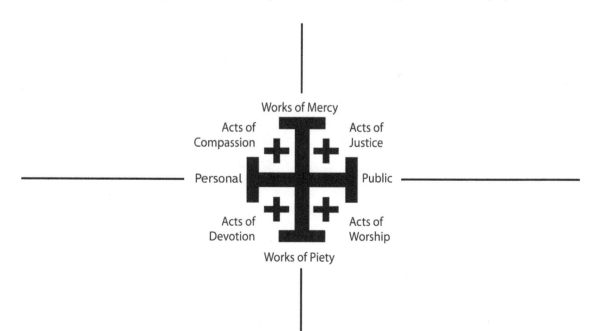

Works of Mercy

Acts of Compassion — Acts of Justice

Personal — Public

Acts of Devotion — Acts of Worship

Works of Piety

A Word from John Wesley

If you ask, "Why then have not all men this faith? all, at least, who conceive it to be so happy a thing? Why do they not believe immediately?"

We answer, (on the Scripture hypothesis,) "It is the gift of God." No man is able to work it in himself. It is a work of omnipotence. It requires no less power thus to quicken a dead soul, than to raise a body that lies in the grave. It is a new creation; and none can create a soul anew, but He who at first created the heavens and the earth.

"An Earnest Appeal to Men of Reason and Religion," 1744; ¶ 9

A Hymn from Charles Wesley

Author of faith, eternal Word,
Whose Spirit breathes the active flame,
Faith, like its finisher and Lord,
Today as yesterday the same.

To thee our humble hearts aspire,
And ask the gift unspeakable:
Increase in us the kindled fire,
In us the work of faith fulfil.

By faith we know thee strong to save
(Save us, a present Saviour thou!)
Whate'er we hope, by faith we have,
Future and past subsisting now.

(*Collection*-1781, #92: 1, 2, 3; SM)

Prayers, Comments & Questions

Steadfast God, you have enriched and enlightened us by the revelation of your eternal Christ. Comfort us in our mortality and strengthen us to walk the path of your desire, so that by word and deed we may manifest the gracious news of your faithfulness and love. Amen.

January Third Sunday after the Epiphany

Preparation for Sunday
Daily: Psalm 27:1-6

26

Thursday
1 Samuel 1:1-20
Galatians 1:11-24

23

Friday
1 Samuel 9:27—10:8
Galatians 2:1-10

24

Saturday
1 Samuel 15:34—16:13
Luke 5:27-32

25

Sunday
Isaiah 9:1-4
Psalm 27:1, 4-9
1 Corinthians 1:10-18
Matthew 4:12-23

Reflection on Sunday
Daily: Psalm 27:7-14

Monday
Judges 6:11-24
Ephesians 5:6-14

27

Tuesday
Judges 7:12-22
Philippians 2:12-18

28

Wednesday
Genesis 49:1-2, 8-13, 21-26
Luke 1:67-79

29

The General Rule of Discipleship
*To witness to Jesus Christ in the world and to follow his teachings
through acts of compassion, justice, worship, and devotion under the guidance of the Holy Spirit.*

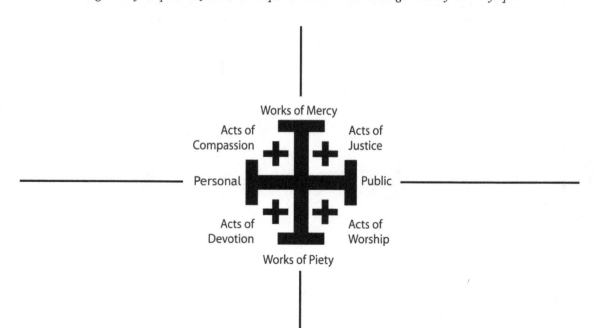

54

A Word from John Wesley

It (faith) is the free gift of God, which he bestows, not on those who are worthy of his favour, not on such as are previously holy, and so fit to be crowned with all the blessings of his goodness; but on the ungodly and unholy; on those who till that hour were fit only for everlasting destruction; those in whom was no good thing, and whose only plea was, "God be merciful to me, a sinner!" No merit, no goodness in man precedes the forgiving love of God. His pardoning mercy supposes nothing in us but a sense of mere sin and misery; and to all who see, and feel, and own their wants, and their utter inability to remove them, God freely gives faith, for the sake of Him in whom he is always "well pleased."

"An Earnest Appeal to Men of Reason and Religion," 1744, ¶ 11

A Hymn from Charles Wesley

To him that in thy name believes
Eternal life with thee is given;
Into himself he all receives—
Pardon, and holiness, and heaven.

The things unknown to feeble sense,
Unseen by reason's glimmering ray,
With strong commanding evidence
Their heavenly origin display.

Faith lends its realizing light,
The clouds disperse, the shadows fly;
Th'Invisible appears in sight,
And God is seen by mortal eye.

(*Collection*-1781, #92: 4, 5, 6; SM)

Prayers, Comments & Questions

God of blazing light, through the power of the cross you shattered our darkness, scattering the fears that bind us and setting us free to live as your children. Give us courage and conviction that we may joyfully turn and follow you into new adventures of faithful service, led by the light that shines through Jesus Christ our Savior. Amen.

Feb 2 Fourth Sunday after the Epiphany

If this Sunday immediately precedes Ash Wednesday, the readings for Sunday and the readings for the surrounding days may be replaced, in those churches observing the Transfiguration on that Sunday, by the readings for the Last Sunday after the Epiphany and the readings for the days surrounding it.

Preparation for Sunday
Daily: Psalm 15

30 **Thursday**
Deuteronomy 16:18-20
1 Peter 3:8-12

31 **Friday**
Deuteronomy 24:17—25:4
1 Timothy 5:17-24

Feb 1 **Saturday**
Micah 3:1-4
John 13:31-35

Sunday
Micah 6:1-8
Psalm 15
1 Corinthians 1:18-31
Matthew 5:1-12

Reflection on Sunday
Daily: Psalm 37:1-17

3 **Monday**
Ruth 1:1-18
Philemon 1-25

4 **Tuesday**
Ruth 2:1-16
James 5:1-6

5 **Wednesday**
Ruth 3:1-13; 4:13-22
Luke 6:17-26

The General Rule of Discipleship
To witness to Jesus Christ in the world and to follow his teachings
through acts of compassion, justice, worship, and devotion under the guidance of the Holy Spirit.

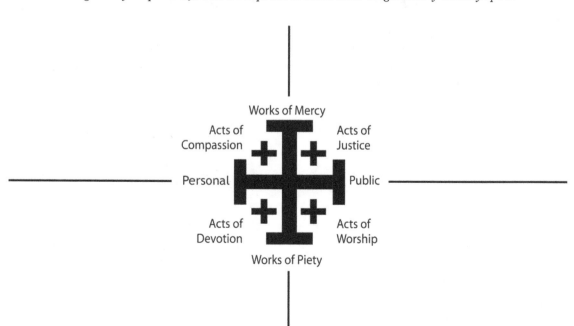

Works of Mercy

Acts of Compassion   Acts of Justice

Personal   Public

Acts of Devotion   Acts of Worship

Works of Piety

A Word from John Wesley

The distinguishing marks of a Methodist are not his opinions of any sort. His assenting to this or that scheme of religion, his embracing any particular set of notions, his espousing the judgment of one man or of another, are all quite wide of the point. Whosoever, therefore, imagines that a Methodist is a man of such or such an opinion, is grossly ignorant of the whole affair; he mistakes the truth totally. We believe, indeed, that "all Scripture is given by the inspiration of God." We believe the written word of God to be the only and sufficient rule both of Christian faith and practice. We believe Christ to be the eternal, supreme God. But as to all opinions which do not strike at the root of Christianity, we think and let think.

"The Character of a Methodist," 1742, ¶ 1

A Hymn from Charles Wesley

Jesu, if still the same thou art,
If all thy promises are sure,
Set up thy kingdom in my heart,
And make me rich, for I am poor:
To me be all thy treasures given,
The kingdom of an inward heaven.

Thou hast pronounced the mourners blest,
And lo! for thee I ever mourn.
I cannot, no, I will not rest
Till thou my only rest return;
Till thou, the Prince of peace, appear,
And I receive the Comforter.

Where is the blessedness bestowed
On all that hunger after thee?
I hunger now, I thirst for God!
See the poor fainting sinner, see,
And satisfy with endless peace,
And fill me with thy righteousness.

(*Collection*-1781, #130:1-3; 88.88.88)

Prayers, Comments & Questions

God our deliverer, you walk with the meek and the poor, the compassionate and those who mourn, and you call us to walk humbly with you. When we are foolish, be our wisdom; when we are weak, be our strength; that, as we learn to do justice and to love mercy, your rule may come as blessing. Amen.

Fifth Sunday after the Epiphany

If this Sunday immediately precedes Ash Wednesday, the readings for Sunday and the readings for the surrounding days may be replaced, in those churches observing the Transfiguration on that Sunday, by the readings for the Last Sunday after the Epiphany and the readings for the days surrounding it.

Preparation for Sunday
Daily: Psalm 112:1-10

Thursday
Deuteronomy 4:1-14
1 John 5:1-5

Friday
Isaiah 29:1-12
James 3:13-18

Saturday
Isaiah 29:13-16
Mark 7:1-8

Sunday
Isaiah 58:1-12
Psalm 112:1-10
1 Corinthians 2:1-16
Matthew 5:13-20

Reflection on Sunday
Daily: Psalm 119:105-112

Monday
2 Kings 22:3-20
Romans 11:2-10

Tuesday
2 Kings 23:1-8, 21-25
2 Corinthians 4:1-12

Wednesday
Proverbs 6:6-23
John 8:12-30

The General Rule of Discipleship
To witness to Jesus Christ in the world and to follow his teachings
through acts of compassion, justice, worship, and devotion under the guidance of the Holy Spirit.

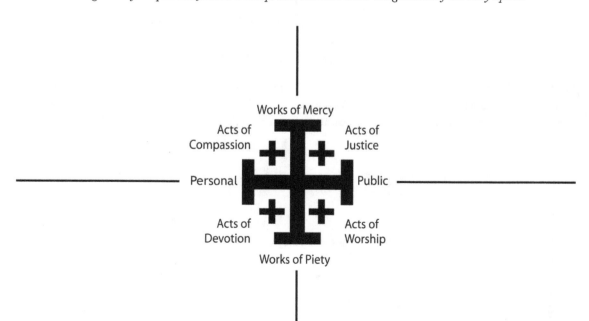

A Word from John Wesley

A Methodist is one who has "the love of God shed abroad in his heart by the Holy Ghost given unto him;" one who "loves the Lord his God with all his heart, and with all his soul, and with all his mind, and with all his strength. God is the joy of his heart, and the desire of his soul; which is constantly crying out, "Whom have I in heaven but thee? and there is none upon earth that I desire beside thee! My God and my all! Thou art the strength of my heart, and my portion for ever!"

"The Character of a Methodist," 1742, ¶ 5

A Hymn from Charles Wesley

Ah, Lord, with trembling I confess,
A gracious soul may fall from grace!
The salt may lose its seas'ning power,
And never, never find it more!

Lest that my fearful case should be,
Each moment knit my soul to thee,
And lead me to the mount above
Through the low vale of humble love.

(*Collection*-1781, #308; LM)

Prayers, Comments & Questions

O God of light, your searching Spirit reveals and illumines your presence in creation. Shine your radiant holiness into our lives, that we may offer our hands and hearts to your work; to heal and shelter, to feed and clothe, to break every yoke and silence evil tongues. Amen.

Sixth Sunday after the Epiphany

If this Sunday immediately precedes Ash Wednesday, the readings for Sunday and the readings for the surrounding days may be replaced, in those churches observing the Transfiguration on that Sunday, by the readings for the Last Sunday after the Epiphany and the readings for the days surrounding it.

Preparation for Sunday
Daily: Psalm 119:1-8

Thursday
Genesis 26:1-5
James 1:12-16

Friday
Leviticus 26:34-46
1 John 2:7-17

Saturday
Deuteronomy 30:1-9a
Matthew 15:1-9

Sunday
Deuteronomy 30:15-20
Psalm 119:1-8
1 Corinthians 3:1-9
Matthew 5:21-37

Reflection on Sunday
Daily: Psalm 119:9-16

Monday
Exodus 20:1-21
James 1:2-8

Tuesday
Deuteronomy 23:21—24:4,
10-15
James 2:1-13

Wednesday
Proverbs 2:1-15
Matthew 19:1-1

The General Rule of Discipleship
*To witness to Jesus Christ in the world and to follow his teachings
through acts of compassion, justice, worship, and devotion under the guidance of the Holy Spirit.*

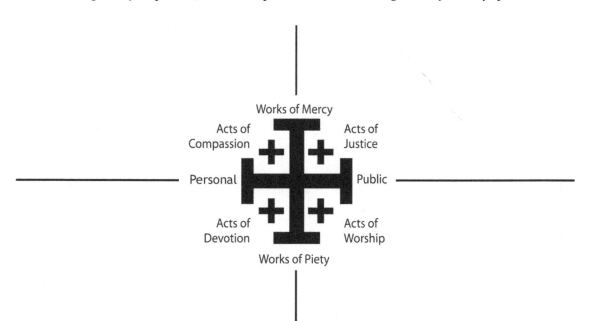

A Word from John Wesley

"There is one Lord," who has now dominion over [Christians]; who has set up his kingdom in their hearts, and reigns over all those that are partakers of this hope. To obey him, to run the way of his commandments, is their glory and joy . . ."

Sermon 74-"On The Church", ¶ 10

A Hymn from Charles Wesley

His love surpassing far
The love of all beneath,
We find within our hearts, and dare
The pointless darts of death.
Stronger than death or hell
The mystic power we prove;
And conqu'rors of the world, we dwell
In heaven, who dwell in love.

We by his Spirit prove
And know the things of God;
The things which freely of his love
He hath on us bestowed:
His Spirit to us he gave,
And dwells in us, we know;
The witness in ourselves we have,
And all his fruits we show.

(*Collection*-1781, #93:3, 4; SMD)

Prayers, Comments & Questions

Divine Gardener, you give growth to our seeds and to the towering forest trees; you raise to abundant life that which seems dead. Teach us to choose blessing and life rather than death, so that we may walk blamelessly, seeking you through reconciliation with all your children. Amen.

Seventh Sunday after the Epiphany

If this Sunday immediately precedes Ash Wednesday, the readings for Sunday and the readings for the surrounding days may be replaced, in those churches observing the Transfiguration on that Sunday, by the readings for the Last Sunday after the Epiphany and the readings for the days surrounding it.

Preparation for Sunday
Daily: Psalm 119:33-40

Thursday 20
Exodus 22:21-27
1 Corinthians 10:23—11:1

Friday 21
Leviticus 6:1-7
Galatians 5:2-6

Saturday 22
Leviticus 24:10-23
Matthew 7:1-12

Sunday 23
Leviticus 19:1-2, 9-18
Psalm 119:33-40
1 Corinthians 3:10-11, 16-23
Matthew 5:38-48

Reflection on Sunday
Daily: Psalm 119:57-64

Monday 24
Proverbs 25:11-22
Romans 12:9-21

Tuesday 25
Genesis 31:1-3, 17-50
Hebrews 12:14-16

Wednesday
Proverbs 3:27-35 26
Luke 18:18-30

The General Rule of Discipleship
To witness to Jesus Christ in the world and to follow his teachings
through acts of compassion, justice, worship, and devotion under the guidance of the Holy Spirit.

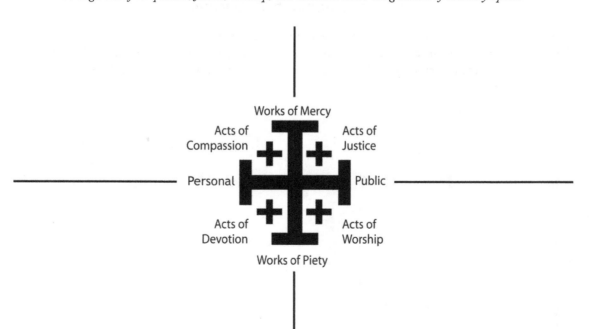

A Word from John Wesley

"There is one faith;" which is the free gift of God, and is the ground of our hope. This is not barely the faith of a Heathen: Namely, a belief that "there is a God," and that he is gracious and just, and, consequently, "a rewarder of them that diligently seek him." Neither is it barely the faith of a devil; though this goes much farther than the former: For the devil believes, and cannot but believe, all that is written both in the Old and New Testament to be true. But it is the faith of St. Thomas, teaching him to say with holy boldness, "My Lord, and my God!" It is the faith which enables every true Christian believer to testify with St. Paul, "The life which I now live, I live by faith in the Son of God, who loved me, and gave himself for me."

Sermon 74-"On The Church", ¶ 11

A Hymn from Charles Wesley

So shall I do thy will below
As angels do above;
The virtue of thy Passion show,
The triumphs of thy love.

Thy love the conquest more than gains;
To all I shall proclaim
Jesus the king, the conqu'ror, reigns—
Bow down to Jesu's name.

(*Collection*-1781, #267: 9 & 10; CM)

Prayers, Comments & Questions

O God most holy, in Jesus Christ you have laid a foundation upon which to build our lives. Help us to follow your perfect law of love, that we may fulfill it and observe it to the end. Amen.

Eighth Sunday after the Epiphany

If this Sunday immediately precedes Ash Wednesday, the readings for Sunday and the readings for the surrounding days may be replaced, in those churches observing the Transfiguration on that Sunday, by the readings for the Last Sunday after the Epiphany and the readings for the days surrounding it.

Preparation for Sunday
Daily: Psalm 131

Thursday
Proverbs 12:22-28
Philippians 2:19-24

Friday
Isaiah 26:1-6
Philippians 2:25-30

Saturday
Isaiah 31:1-9
Luke 11:14-23

Sunday
Isaiah 49:8-16a
Psalm 131
1 Corinthians 4:1-5
Matthew 6:24-34

Reflection on Sunday
Daily: Psalm 104

Monday
Deuteronomy 32:1-14
Hebrews 10:32-39

Tuesday
1 Kings 17:1-16
1 Corinthians 4:6-21

Wednesday
Isaiah 66:7-13
Luke 12:22-31

The General Rule of Discipleship
To witness to Jesus Christ in the world and to follow his teachings
through acts of compassion, justice, worship, and devotion under the guidance of the Holy Spirit.

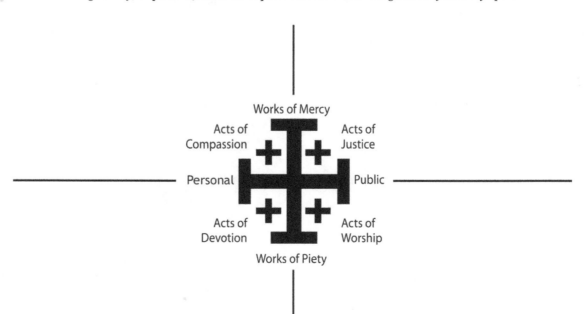

Works of Mercy

Acts of Compassion — Acts of Justice

Personal — Public

Acts of Devotion — Acts of Worship

Works of Piety

A Word from John Wesley

"There is one baptism;" which is the outward sign our one Lord has been pleased to appoint, of all that inward and spiritual grace which he is continually bestowing upon his Church. It is likewise a precious means, whereby this faith and hope are given to those that diligently seek him.

Sermon 74: "On The Church", ¶ 12

A Hymn from Charles Wesley

Shall I, for fear of feeble man,
The Spirit's course in me restrain?
Or undismayed in deed and word,
Be a true witness to my Lord?

Awed by a mortal's frown, shall I
Conceal the Word of God most high?
How then before thee shall I dare
To stand, or how thine anger bear?

Shall I, to soothe th'unholy throng,
Soften thy truths, and smooth my tongue?
To gain earth's gilded toys, or flee
The cross, endured, my God, by thee?

(*Collection*-1781, #270: 1-3; LM)

Prayers, Comments & Questions

God of tender care, like a mother you never forget your children, but comfort and quiet those who are restless and fearful; like a father you know already what we need. In all our anxiety, give us the spirit of trust; in all our worry, give us faithful hearts; that in confidence and calm we may seek the kingdom of Christ where your holy will of peace and justice has been made known. Amen.

March

Ninth Sunday after the Epiphany

The readings that follow are for churches whose calendar requires this Sunday, and who do not observe the last Sunday after the Epiphany as Transfiguration.

Preparation for Sunday
Daily: Psalm 31:1-5, 19-24

Thursday
Exodus 24:1-8
Romans 2:17-29

Friday
Deuteronomy 30:1-5
Romans 9:6-13

Saturday
Amos 2:6-11
Matthew 7:1-6

Sunday
Deuteronomy 11:18-21, 26-28
Psalm 31:1-5, 19-24
Romans 1:16-17; 3:22b-31
Matthew 7:21-29

Reflection on Sunday
Daily: Psalm 52

Monday
Joshua 8:30-35
Romans 2:1-11

Tuesday
Joshua 24:1-2, 11-28
Romans 3:9-22a

Wednesday
Job 28:12-28
Matthew 7:13-20

The General Rule of Discipleship
*To witness to Jesus Christ in the world and to follow his teachings
through acts of compassion, justice, worship, and devotion under the guidance of the Holy Spirit.*

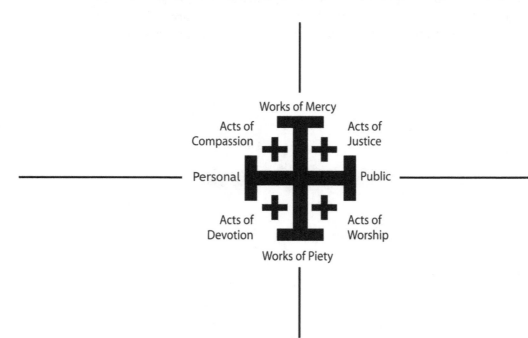

A Word from John Wesley

"There is one God and Father of all" that have the Spirit of adoption, which "crieth in their hearts, Abba, Father;" which "witnesseth" continually "with their spirits," that they are the children of God: "Who is above all,"—the Most High, the Creator, the Sustainer, the Governor of the whole universe: "And through all,"—pervading all space; filling heaven and earth: "And in you all,"—in a peculiar manner living in you, that are one body, by one Spirit:

Making your souls his loved abode,
The temples of indwelling God.

Sermon 74: "On The Church", ¶ 13

A Hymn from Charles Wesley

I rest in thine almighty power;
The name of Jesus is a tower
That hides my life above!
Thou canst, thou wilt my helper be;
My confidence is all in thee,
The faithful God of love.

While still to thee for help I call
Thou wilt not suffer me to fall,
Thou canst not let me sin;
And thou shalt give me power to pray
Till all my sins are purged away,
And all thy mind brought in.

(*Collection*-1781, #273: 3 & 4; 886.886)

Prayers, Comments & Questions

O Lord, faithful God, you are our rock and refuge. Help us to hear your word as truth and to act on it in faith, that all may come to know your love. Amen.

Last Sunday after the Epiphany
Transfiguration Sunday

Preparation for Sunday
Daily: Psalm 2

Thursday
Exodus 6:2-9
Hebrews 8:1-7

Friday
Exodus 19:9b-25
Hebrews 11:23-28

Saturday
1 Kings 21:20-29
Mark 9:9-13

Sunday
Exodus 24:12-18
Psalm 2
2 Peter 1:16-21
Matthew 17:1-9

Reflection on Sunday
Daily: Psalm 78:17-20, 52-55

Monday
Exodus 33:7-23
Acts 7:30-34

Tuesday
1 Kings 19:9-18
Romans 11:1-6

Ash Wednesday
Joel 2:1-2, 12-17
Psalm 51:1-17
2 Corinthians 5:20b—6:10
Matthew 6:1-6, 16-21

The General Rule of Discipleship
*To witness to Jesus Christ in the world and to follow his teachings
through acts of compassion, justice, worship, and devotion under the guidance of the Holy Spirit.*

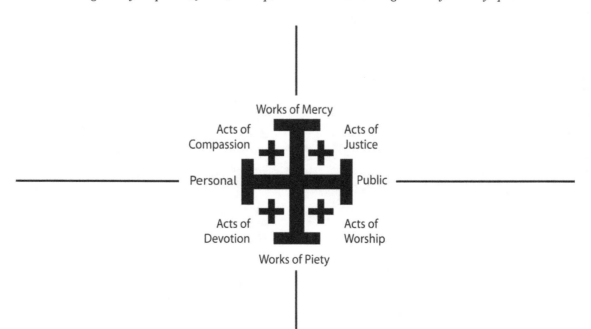

A Word from John Wesley

Yea, suppose God has now thoroughly cleansed our heart, and scattered the last remains of sin; yet how can we be sensible enough of our own helplessness, our utter inability to all good, unless we are every hour, yea, every moment, endued with power from on high? Who is able to think one good thought, or to form one good desire, unless by that almighty power which worketh in us both to will and to do of his good pleasure? We have need, even in this state of grace, to be thoroughly and continually penetrated with a sense of this. Otherwise we shall be in perpetual danger of robbing God of his honour, by glorying in something we have received, as though we had not received it.

Sermon 74: "On The Church", ¶ 22

A Hymn from Charles Wesley

I will not let thee go, unless
Thou tell thy name to me;
With all thy great salvation bless,
And make me all like thee.

Then let me on the mountain top
Behold thy open face,
Where faith in sight is swallowed up,
And prayer in endless praise.

(*Collection*-1781, #288: 5 & 6; CM)

Prayers, Comments & Questions

O God of the covenant, the cloud of your splendor and the fire of your love revealed your Son on the mountain heights. Transform our lives in his image, write your law of love on our hearts, and make us prophets of your glory, that we may lead others into your presence. Amen.

Ash Wednesday
O God, you delight not in pomp and show, but in a humble and contrite heart. Overturn our love of worldly possessions and fix our hearts more firmly on you, that, having nothing, we may yet possess everything, a treasure stored up for us in heaven. Amen.

Lent

Forming Disciples Who Live as Jesus Lived

The primary purpose of Lent, from its beginnings, has been to provide a period of intense formation for those preparing to take on the covenant of baptism with the baptized, with baptism celebrated at Easter. Over time, as the early church's extensive three-year system of formation (called the catechumenate) fell into disuse, Lent became in practice primarily a time for penitence and increased acts of self-discipline, as well as, in some ways, particularly among Protestants, a kind of "extended Holy Week" for contemplating the suffering of Jesus.

With the renewal of the Christian Year brought about for Roman Catholics in Vatican II (early 1960s) and for Protestants coinciding with the development of the Revised Common Lectionary (1992), more and more Western Christians have recovered the idea, if not entirely the practices, of Lent as a season of preparation for baptism, reconciliation for the estranged, and final preparation for confirmation or reaffirmation by those baptized who are deemed ready to take the vows of baptism for themselves for the first time or in a deeper way.

Consequently, the readings you will experience on Sundays and weekdays during Lent are much more about how Jesus teaches his disciples to follow him and not about the sufferings of Jesus or his execution per se. And every year the Sunday readings correspond with key elements of the baptismal vows. If your congregation is not already providing accountable small groups to read and explore the implications of these readings, Sunday and/or daily, for living as the baptized, let me encourage you to gather a few Christian friends and create your own. Consider meeting face to face at least once weekly.

When you gather, read one of the gospel readings aloud three times, *lectio continua* style, paying attention the first time to what catches your attention, the second to what the thing that caught your attention is calling you to do, and the third to how you will respond in obedience to do it. Then share what you have gleaned from your reading with others in your small group. Decide how you will help each other be obedient to what you each have heard during the coming week.

Rev. Taylor Burton-Edwards

March

1 March

First Sunday in Lent

Preparation for Sunday
Daily: Psalm 51

19 **Thursday**
Jonah 3:1-10
Romans 1:1-7

20 **Friday**
Jonah 4:1-11
Romans 1:8-17

21 **Saturday**
Isaiah 58:1-12
Matthew 18:1-7

22 **Sunday**
Genesis 2:15-17; 3:1-7
Psalm 32
Romans 5:12-19
Matthew 4:1-11

Reflection on Sunday
Daily: Psalm 32

23 **Monday**
1 Kings 19:1-8
Hebrews 2:10-18

March 3

24 **Tuesday**
Genesis 4:1-16
Hebrews 4:14—5:10

25 **Wednesday**
Exodus 34:1-9, 27-28
Matthew 18:10-14

4

The General Rule of Discipleship
*To witness to Jesus Christ in the world and to follow his teachings
through acts of compassion, justice, worship, and devotion under the guidance of the Holy Spirit.*

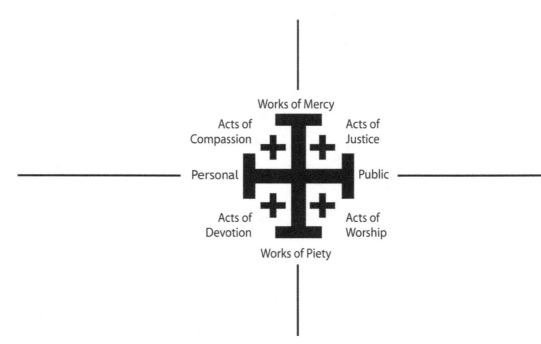

Works of Mercy

Acts of Compassion — Acts of Justice

Personal — Public

Acts of Devotion — Acts of Worship

Works of Piety

A Word from John Wesley

Repentance frequently means an inward change, a change of mind from sin to holiness. But we now speak of it in a quite different sense, as it is one kind of self-knowledge, the knowing ourselves sinners, yea, guilty, helpless sinners, even though we know we are children of God.

Sermon 14: "The Repentance of Believers", § I:1

A Hymn from Charles Wesley

My sufferings all to thee are known,
Tempted in every point like me;
Regard my grief, regard thy own;
Jesus, remember Calvary!

O call to mind thy earnest prayers!
Thy agony and sweat of blood!
Thy strong and bitter cries and tears!
Thy mortal groan, 'My God, my God!

(*Collection*-1781, #155: 1 & 2; LM)

Prayers, Comments & Questions

God of mercy, your word was the sure defense of Jesus in this time of testing. Minister to us in the wilderness of our temptation, that we who have been set free from sin by Christ may serve you well into life everlasting. Amen.

March 8 ## Second Sunday in Lent

Preparation for Sunday
Daily: Psalm 121

26 **Thursday** 5
Isaiah 51:1-3
2 Timothy 1:3-7

27 **Friday** 6
Micah 7:18-20
Romans 3:21-31

28 **Saturday** 7
Isaiah 51:4-8
Luke 7:1-10

29 **Sunday**
Genesis 12:1-4a
Psalm 121
Romans 4:1-5, 13-17
John 3:1-17

Reflection on Sunday
Daily: Psalm 128

30 **Monday** 9
Numbers 21:4-9
Hebrews 3:1-6

31 **Tuesday** 10
Isaiah 65:17-25
Romans 4:6-13

April 1

Wednesday 11
Ezekiel 36:22-32
John 7:53—8:11

The General Rule of Discipleship
To witness to Jesus Christ in the world and to follow his teachings
through acts of compassion, justice, worship, and devotion under the guidance of the Holy Spirit.

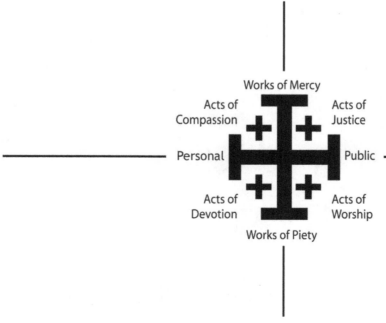

A Word from John Wesley

For it is seldom long before [the repentant person] who imagined all sin was gone, feels there is still *pride* in his heart. He is convinced both that in many respects he has thought of himself more highly than he ought to think, and that he has taken to himself the praise of something he had received, and gloried in it as though he had not received it; and yet he knows he is in the favour of God. He cannot, and ought not to, "cast away his confidence." "The Spirit" still "witnesses with" his "spirit, that he is a child of God."

Sermon 14: "The Repentance of Believers", § I:3

A Hymn from Charles Wesley

Who can sound the depths unknown
Of thy redeeming grace?
Grace that gave thine only Son
To save a ruined race!
Millions of transgressors poor
Thou hast for Jesu's sake forgiven,
Made them of thy favour sure,
And snatched from hell to heaven.

Millions more thou ready art
To save, and to forgive;
Every soul, and every heart
Of man thou wouldst receive.
Father, now accept of mine,
Which now through Christ I offer thee:
Tell me now, in love divine,
That thou hast pardoned me!

(*Collection*-1781, #236:3 & 4; 76.76 D)

Prayers, Comments & Questions

God of amazing compassion, lover of our wayward race, you bring to birth a pilgrim people, and call us to be a blessing for ourselves and all the world. We pray for grace to take your generous gift and step with courage on this holy path, confident in the radiant life that is your plan for us, made known and given in Jesus Christ our Lord. Amen.

Third Sunday in Lent

April *March* 15

Preparation for Sunday
Daily: Psalm 95

Thursday 12
Exodus 16:1-8
Colossians 1:15-23

Friday 13
Exodus 16:9-21
Ephesians 2:11-22

Saturday 14
Exodus 16:27-35
John 4:1-6

Sunday
Exodus 17:1-7
Psalm 95
Romans 5:1-11
John 4:5-42

Reflection on Sunday
Daily: Psalm 81

Monday 16
Genesis 24:1-27
2 John 1-13

Tuesday 17
Genesis 29:1-14
1 Corinthians 10:1-4

Wednesday 18
Jeremiah 2:4-13
John 7:14-31, 37-39

The General Rule of Discipleship
*To witness to Jesus Christ in the world and to follow his teachings
through acts of compassion, justice, worship, and devotion under the guidance of the Holy Spirit.*

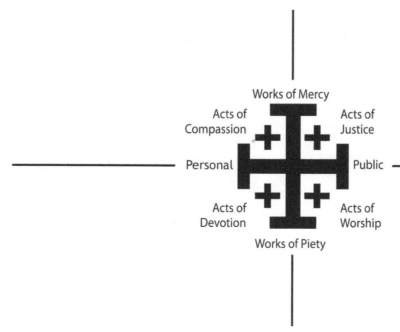

A Word from John Wesley

Now self-will, as well as pride, is a species of *idolatry* and both are directly contrary to the love of God. The same observation may be made concerning the *love of the world*. But this likewise even true believers are liable to feel in themselves; and every one of them does feel it, more or less, sooner or later, in one branch or another. . . . Nay, if he does not continually watch and pray, he may find *lust* reviving; yea, and thrusting sore at him that he may fall, till he has scarce any strength left in him.

Sermon 14: "The Repentance of Believers", § I:5

A Hymn from Charles Wesley

Jesus, the gift divine I know,
The gift divine I ask of thee;
That living water now bestow,
Thy Spirit and thyself on me.
Thou, Lord, of life the fountain art:
Now let me find thee in my heart!

Thee let me drink, and thirst no more
For drops of finite happiness;
Spring up, O well, in heavenly power,
In streams of pure, perennial peace,
In peace, that none can take away,
In joy, which shall forever stay.

(*Collection*-1781, #354:1 & 2; LMD)

Prayers, Comments & Questions

Enduring Presence, goal and guide, you go before and await our coming. Only our thirst compels us beyond complaint to conversation, beyond rejection to relationship. Pour your love into our hearts, that, refreshed and renewed, we may invite others to the living water given to us in Jesus Christ our Lord. Amen.

April

Fourth Sunday in Lent

Preparation for Sunday
Daily: Psalm 23

22

Sunday
1 Samuel 16:1-13
Psalm 23
Ephesians 5:8-14
John 9:1-41

Reflection on Sunday
Daily: Psalm 146

19

Thursday
1 Samuel 15:10-21
Ephesians 4:25-32

13 **Monday**
Isaiah 59:9-19
Acts 9:1-20

20

Friday
1 Samuel 15:22-31
Ephesians 5:1-9

24 **Tuesday**
Isaiah 42:14-21
Colossians 1:9-14

21

Saturday
1 Samuel 15:32-34
John 1:1-9

25 **Wednesday**
Isaiah 60:17-22
Matthew 9:27-34

The General Rule of Discipleship
*To witness to Jesus Christ in the world and to follow his teachings
through acts of compassion, justice, worship, and devotion under the guidance of the Holy Spirit.*

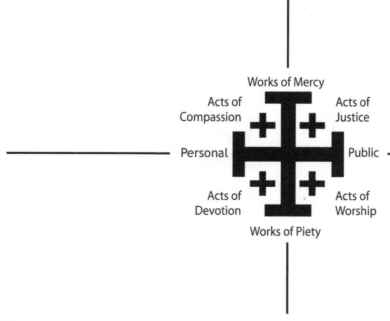

Works of Mercy

Acts of Compassion   Acts of Justice

Personal   Public

Acts of Devotion   Acts of Worship

Works of Piety

A Word from John Wesley

Covetousness, in every kind and degree, is certainly as contrary . . . to the love of God; whether, the love of money, which is too frequently "the root of all evil;" or a desire of having more, or increasing in substance. And how few, even of the real children of God, are entirely free from both!

Sermon 14: "The Repentance of Believers", § I:9

A Hymn from Charles Wesley

Ye thirsty for God,
To Jesus give ear;
And take through his blood
A power to draw near;
His kind invitation
Ye sinners embrace,
The sense of salvation
Accepting through grace.

O Saviour of all,
Thy word we believe,
And come at thy call,
Thy grace to receive;
The blessing is given
Wherever thou art;
The earnest of heaven
Is love in the heart.

(*Collection*-1781, #10:1& 3; 55.55.65.65)

Prayers, Comments & Questions

Discerner of hearts, you look beneath our outward appearance and see your image in each of us. Banish in us the blindness that prevents us from recognizing truth, so we may see the world through your eyes and with the compassion of Jesus Christ who redeems us. Amen.

Fifth Sunday in Lent

Preparation for Sunday
Daily: Psalm 130

Thursday
Ezekiel 1:1-3; 2:8—3:3
Revelation 10:1-11

Friday
Ezekiel 33:10-16
Revelation 11:15-19

Saturday
Ezekiel 36:8-15
Luke 24:44-53

Sunday
Ezekiel 37:1-14
Psalm 130
Romans 8:6-11
John 11:1-45

Reflecting on Sunday
Daily: Psalm 143

Monday
1 Kings 17:17-24
Acts 20:7-12

Tuesday
2 Kings 4:18-37
Ephesians 2:1-10

Wednesday
Jeremiah 32:1-9, 36-41
Matthew 22:23-33

The General Rule of Discipleship
To witness to Jesus Christ in the world and to follow his teachings
through acts of compassion, justice, worship, and devotion under the guidance of the Holy Spirit.

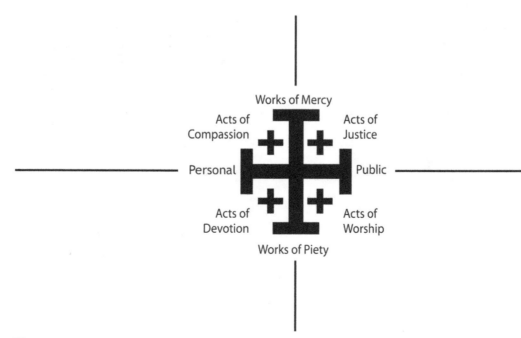

A Word from John Wesley

But we should likewise be convinced, that as sin remains in our hearts, so it *cleaves* to all our words and actions. Indeed it is to be feared, that many of our words are more than mixed with sin; that they are sinful altogether; for such undoubtedly is all *uncharitable conversation;* all which does not spring from brotherly love; all which does not agree with that golden rule, "What ye would that others should do to you, even so do unto them." Of this kind is all backbiting, all tale-bearing, all whispering, all evil-speaking, that is, repeating the faults of absent persons; for none would have others repeat his faults when he is absent. Now how few are there, even among believers, who are in no degree guilty of this; who steadily observe the good old rule, "Of the dead and the absent, nothing but good!"

Sermon 14: "The Repentance of Believers", § I:11

A Hymn from Charles Wesley

There for me the Saviour stands,
Shows his wounds, and spreads his hands!
God is love! I know, I feel.
Jesus weeps, and loves me still!

Jesus, answer from above:
Is not all thy nature love?
Wilt thou not the wrong forget?
Suffer me to kiss thy feet?

(*Collection*-1781, #162:8 & 9; 77.77)

Prayers, Comments & Questions

God of all consolation and compassion, your Son comforted the grieving sisters, Martha and Mary; your breath alone brings life to dry bones and weary souls. Pour out your Spirit upon us, that we may face despair and death with the hope of resurrection and faith in the One who called Lazarus forth from the grave. Amen.

Sixth Sunday in Lent
Passion/Palm Sunday

Herald 5

Preparation for Sunday
Daily: Psalm 31:9-16

Thursday
1 Samuel 16:11-13
Philippians 1:1-11

Friday
Job 13:13-19
Philippians 1:21-30

Saturday
Lamentations 3:55-66
Mark 10:32-34

Sunday
Liturgy of the Palms
Psalm 118:1-2, 19-29
Matthew 21:1-11

Liturgy of the Passion
Isaiah 50:4-9a
Psalm 31:9-16
Philippians 2:5-11
Matthew 26:14—27:66

The General Rule of Discipleship
To witness to Jesus Christ in the world and to follow his teachings
through acts of compassion, justice, worship, and devotion under the guidance of the Holy Spirit.

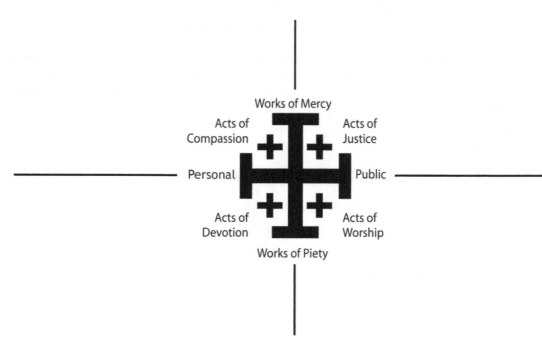

A Word from John Wesley

Again: How many *sins of omission* are they chargeable with! We know the words of the Apostle: "To him that knoweth to do good, and doeth it not, to him it is sin." But do they not know a thousand instances, wherein they might have done good, to enemies, to strangers, to their brethren, either with regard to their bodies or their souls, and they did it not? How many omissions have they been guilty of, in their duty toward God! How many opportunities of communicating, of hearing his word, of public or private prayer, have they neglected!

Sermon 14: "The Repentance of Believers", § I:14

A Hymn from Charles Wesley

Who hath done the direful deed,
Hath crucified my God?
Curses on his guilty head,
Who spilt that precious blood.
Worthy is the wretch to die;
Self-condemned, alas, is he!—
I have sold my Saviour; I
Have nailed him to the tree.

Yet thy wrath I cannot fear,
Thou gentle, bleeding Lamb!
By thy judgment I am clear;
Healed by thy stripes I am:
Thou for me a curse wast made,
That I might in thee be blest;
Thou hast my full ransom paid,
And in thy wounds I rest.

(*Collection*-1781, #206:4 & 5; 76.76 D)

Prayers, Comments & Questions

Merciful God, your strength and courage pour forth to sustain the witness of your faithful people. Awaken in us the humility to serve wherever creation is broken and in need, that we may follow in the way of our brother, Jesus, die as he did to all that separates us from you, and with him be raised to new life. Amen.

Holy Week

The Cost of Discipleship and Salvation

Lent moves into Holy Week beginning with Passion/Palm Sunday. This is the time we remember the final week of Jesus in Jerusalem, his last actions with his disciples, his arrest, his trial, his torture, and his execution. The daily readings (Monday through Saturday) are the same all three years, established by long tradition. And these are readings intended to be read and reflected upon in gathered community. Many congregations will have planned gatherings for worship on Maundy Thursday and Good Friday. Fewer may be likely to gather for the solemn vigil of Holy Saturday morning or the other weekdays.

The formational power of this week is greatly enhanced if you do gather every day in some way. Perhaps you may find a time each evening to meet in homes, or a "third place," or perhaps you may decide to gather "virtually" through an online venue such as Skype, Facebook, or Twitter. While during Lent the focus of the readings was to commit to what you might do, during Holy Week the purpose is simply to let them sink in and allow the readings to work their work in your gathered community. Read the scriptures. Pray for the church and the world. Bid each other the peace of Christ. And continue to watch and pray for what the Spirit will put to death and bring to new life in each of you.

Rev. Taylor Burton-Edwards

Monday

Isaiah 42:1-9
Psalm 36:5-11
Hebrews 9:11-15
John 12:1-11

Collect for Monday of Holy Week

God of steadfast love, light of the blind and liberator of the oppressed, we see your holy purpose in the tender compassion of Jesus, who calls us into new and living friendship with you. May we, who take shelter in the shadow of your wings, be filled with the grace of his tender caring; may we, who stumble in selfish darkness, see your glory in the light of his self-giving. We ask this through him whose suffering is victorious, Jesus Christ our Savior. Amen.

Tuesday

Isaiah 49:1-7
Psalm 71:1-14
1 Corinthians 1:18-31
John 12:20-36

Collect for Tuesday of Holy Week

Holy and immortal God, from earliest times you have named us and called us into discipleship. Teach us to follow the One whose light scatters the darkness of our world, that we may walk as children of the light. Amen.

Wednesday

Isaiah 50:4-9a
Psalm 70
Hebrews 12:1-3
John 13:21-32

Collect for Wednesday of Holy Week

Troubled God, in every generation you call your people to contend against the brutality of sin and betrayal. Keep us steadfast even in our fear and uncertainty, that we may follow where Jesus has led the way. Amen.

The Three Days

Holy Thursday

Exodus 12:1-14
Psalm 116:1-2, 12-19
1 Corinthians 11:23-26
John 13:1-17, 31b-35

Collect for Holy Thursday

Eternal God, in the sharing of a meal your Son established a new covenant for all people, and in the washing of feet he showed us the dignity of service. Grant that by the power of your Holy Spirit these signs of our life in faith may speak again to our hearts, feed our spirits, and refresh our bodies. Amen.

Good Friday

Isaiah 52:13—53:12
Psalm 22
Hebrews 10:16-25
John 18:1—19:42

Collect for Good Friday

Grieving God, on the cross your Son embraced death even as he had embraced life: faithfully and with good courage. Grant that we who have been born out of his wounded side may hold fast to our faith in him exalted and may find mercy in all times of need. Amen.

Holy Saturday

Job 14:1-14
Psalm 31:1-4, 15-16
1 Peter 4:1-8
Matthew 27:57-66

Collect for Holy Saturday

Eternal God, rock and refuge: with roots grown old in the earth, river beds run dry, and flowers withered in the field, we wait for revival and release. Abide with us until we come alive in the sunrise of your glory. Amen.

Hymn for Holy Week

O Love divine! What hast thou done!
Th'immortal God hath died for me!
The Father's co-eternal Son
Bore all my sins upon the tree:
Th'immortal God for me hath died,
My Lord, my Love is crucified.

Behold him, all ye that pass by,
The bleeding Prince of life and peace!
Come see, ye worms, your Maker die,
And say, was ever grief like his?
Come, feel with me his blood applied:
My Lord, my Love is crucified.

Is crucified for me and you,
To bring us rebels back to God;
Believe, believe the record true,
Ye all are bought with Jesu's blood:
Pardon for all flows from his side:
My Lord, my Love is crucified.

Then let us sit beneath his cross,
And gladly catch the healing stream,
All things for him account but loss,
And give up all our hearts to him;
Of nothing think or speak beside,
'My Lord, my Love is crucified'.

(*Collection*-1781, #27, 88.88.88)

Easter Season

Teaching and Preparing to Unleash Salvation

The first service of Easter is full of readings! This is the Great Vigil of Easter, offered after sundown on Saturday night. It is a powerful service of Fire, Word, Water, and Table. We light the new fire, signifying the light of Christ overcoming the world. We rehearse the story of God's salvation, from creation and exodus to the resurrection of Christ. We exult in Alleluias. We baptize those who have been preparing during Lent and vigiling in prayer with us during Holy Week. And we celebrate the feast of our redemption around the Lord's Table. If your congregation does not yet celebrate this amazing and ancient Christian service, find one that does (most Episcopal, Roman Catholic, and many Lutheran congregations will!) and take folks with you, including your pastor, so they may see, hear, smell, taste, and touch, and perhaps develop plans to bring others or create one for your congregation next year.

Easter, the Season of the Passover of our Lord, begins with a bang! And it concludes with another one, fifty days later at Pentecost, when we celebrate the coming of the Holy Spirit on the early Christians long ago, and all the ways the Spirit is moving among us here and now.

Between these days of celebration are weeks of further formation so that your celebration, come Pentecost, may be full indeed. Easter Season is a time especially for helping the newly baptized with all the baptized grow in their understanding of Christian doctrine and to identify their gifts and callings for ministry in Christ's name. On Easter, both at the Great Vigil and again on Sunday morning, we exult in the resurrection of Jesus Christ from the dead. On Pentecost, we exult in what the Spirit is doing in the lives of those reborn or recommitted, and we bless and commission them for their ministries among us. And in the weeks between, in Sunday and in daily readings, we prepare ourselves to grow in our knowledge and love of God, and to sharpen our own passions and skills for ministry in Christ's name and the Spirit's power.

Rev. Taylor Burton-Edwards

April 12

Resurrection of the Lord

Easter Sunday Morning
Acts 10:34-43
Psalm 118:1-2, 14-24
Colossians 3:1-4
John 20:1-18
or
Matthew 28:1-10

Evening
Isaiah 25:6-9
Psalm 114
1 Corinthians 5:6b-8
Luke 24:13-49

Reflection on Sunday
Daily: Psalm 118:1-2, 14-24

Monday *13*
Exodus 14:10-31; 15:20-21
Colossians 3:5-11

14 **Tuesday**
Exodus 15:1-18
Colossians 3:12-17

Wednesday *15*
Joshua 3:1-17
Matthew 28:1-10

The General Rule of Discipleship
*To witness to Jesus Christ in the world and to follow his teachings
through acts of compassion, justice, worship, and devotion under the guidance of the Holy Spirit.*

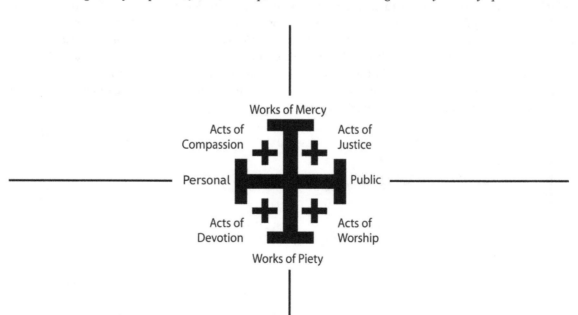

Works of Mercy

Acts of Compassion · Acts of Justice

Personal · Public

Acts of Devotion · Acts of Worship

Works of Piety

A Word from John Wesley

Justification implies only a relative, the new birth a real, change. God in justifying us does something *for* us; in begetting us again, he does the work *in* us. The former changes our outward relation to God, so that of enemies we become children; by the latter our inmost souls are changed, so that of sinners we become saints. The one restores us to the favour, the other to the image, of God. The one is the taking away the guilt, the other the taking away the power, of sin: So that, although they are joined together in point of time, yet are they of wholly distinct natures.

Sermon 19: The Great Privilege of Those That Are Born of God, ¶ 2

A Hymn from Charles Wesley

Sinners, dismiss your fear,
The joyful tidings hear!
This the word that Jesus said,
O believe, and feel it true,
Christ is risen from the dead,
Lives the Lord who died for you!

Knowest thou not where to find
The savior of mankind?
He hath borne himself away,
He from death himself hath freed,
He on the third glorious day,
Rose triumphant from the dead.

He comes his own to claim,
He calls thee by thy name:
Drooping soul, rejoice, rejoice,
See him there to life restored!
Mary—know thy Saviour's voice,
Hear it, and reply "My Lord."

(*Hymns for Our Lord's Resurrection*—1746, #2:1, 4, & 6, 66.77.77)

Prayers, Comments & Questions

Resurrecting God, you conquered death and opened the gates of life everlasting. In the power of the Holy Spirit, raise us with Christ that we, too, may proclaim healing and peace to the nations. Amen.

April 19 Second Sunday of Easter

Preparation for Sunday
Daily: Psalm 16

16 Thursday
Song of Solomon 2:8-15
Colossians 4:2-5

17 Friday
Song of Solomon 5:9—6:3
1 Corinthians 15:1-11

18 Saturday
Song of Solomon 8:6-7
John 20:11-20

Sunday
Acts 2:14a, 22-32
Psalm 16
1 Peter 1:3-9
John 20:19-31

Reflection on Sunday
Daily: Psalm 114

20 Monday
Judges 6:36-40
1 Corinthians 15:12-20

21 Tuesday
Jonah 1:1-17 *1107*
1 Corinthians 15:19-28

22 Wednesday
Jonah 2:1-10
Matthew 12:38-42

The General Rule of Discipleship
*To witness to Jesus Christ in the world and to follow his teachings
through acts of compassion, justice, worship, and devotion under the guidance of the Holy Spirit.*

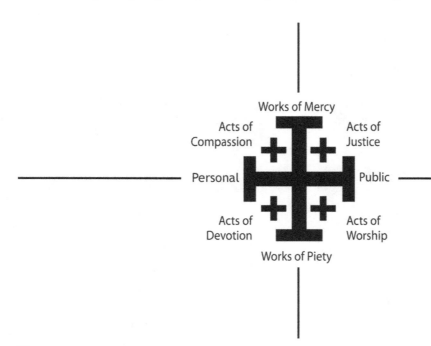

92

A Word from John Wesley

And, in general, from all the passages of holy writ wherein this expression, "the being born of God," occurs, we may learn that it implies not barely the being baptized, or any outward change whatever; but a vast inward change, a change wrought in the soul, by the operation of the Holy Ghost; a change in the whole manner of our existence; for, from the moment we are born of God, we live in quite another manner than we did before; we are, as it were, in another world.

Sermon 19: The Great Privilege of Those That Are Born of God, §I.1

A Hymn from Charles Wesley

All ye who seek the Lord who died,
Your God for sinners crucified,
Prevent the earliest dawn, and com
To worship at his sacred tomb.

While thus ye love your souls t'employ,
Your sorrow shall be turned to joy:
Now, now let all your grief be o'er!
Believe, and ye shall weep no more.

Haste then, ye souls that first believe,
Who dare the gospel word receive,
Your faith with joyful hearts confess,
Be bold, be Jesus' witnesses.

(*Hymns for Our Lord's Resurrection*—1746, 1:1, 3, &11, 88.88)

Prayers, Comments & Questions

Blessed are you, O God of our Lord Jesus Christ, in whom we receive the legacy of a living hope, born again not only from his death but also from his resurrection. May we who have received forgiveness of sins through the Holy Spirit live to set others free, until, at length, we enter the inheritance that is imperishable and unfading, where Christ lives and reigns with you and the same Spirit. Amen.

April

Third Sunday of Easter

26

Preparation for Sunday
Daily: Psalm 116:1-4, 12-19

23 **Thursday**
Isaiah 25:1-5
1 Peter 1:8b-12

24 **Friday**
Isaiah 26:1-4
1 Peter 1:13-16

25 **Saturday**
Isaiah 25:6-9
Luke 14:12-14

Sunday
Acts 2:14a, 36-41
Psalm 116:1-4, 12-19
1 Peter 1:17-23
Luke 24:13-35

Reflection on Sunday
Daily: Psalm 134

27 **Monday**
Genesis 18:1-14
1 Peter 1:23-25

28 **Tuesday**
Proverbs 8:32—9:6
1 Peter 2:1-3

Wednesday
Exodus 24:1-11
John 21:1-14

The General Rule of Discipleship
*To witness to Jesus Christ in the world and to follow his teachings
through acts of compassion, justice, worship, and devotion under the guidance of the Holy Spirit.*

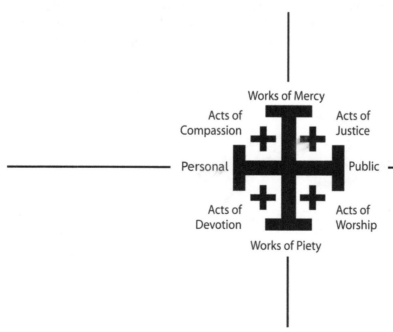

Works of Mercy

Acts of Compassion

Acts of Justice

Personal

Public

Acts of Devotion

Acts of Worship

Works of Piety

A Word from John Wesley

The reason why he that is not yet born is wholly a stranger to the visible world, is, not because it is afar off; (it is very nigh; it surrounds him on every side;) but, partly, because he has not those senses, they are not yet opened in his soul, whereby alone it is possible to hold commerce with the material world; and partly, because so thick a veil is cast between, through which he can discern nothing.

Sermon 19: The Great Privilege of Those That Are Born of God, §I.4

A Hymn from Charles Wesley

Come then, thou prophet of the Lord,
Thou great interpreter divine,
Explain thine own transmitted Word;
To teach, and to inspire is thine,
Thou only cast thyself reveal,
Open the book, and loose the seal.

Come in, with thy disciples sit,
Nor suffer us to ask in vain,
Nourish us, Lord, with living meat.
Our souls with heavenly bread sustain;
Break to us now the mystic bread,
And bid us on thy body feed.

Honour the means ordained by thee,
The great unbloody sacrifice,
The deep tremendous mystery;
Thyself in our in-lightened eyes
Now in the broken bread make known,
And show us thou art all our own.

(*Hymns for Our Lord's Resurrection*—1746, #6:1, 5, & 6; 88.88.88)

Prayers, Comments & Questions

Elusive God, companion on the way, you walk behind, beside, beyond; you catch us unawares. Break through the disillusionment and despair clouding our vision, that, with wide-eyed wonder, we may find our way and journey on as messengers of your good news. Amen.

May

Fourth Sunday of Easter

3

Preparation for Sunday
Daily: Psalm 23

30 **Thursday**
Exodus 2:15b-25 ✓
1 Peter 2:9-12

1 **Friday**
Exodus 3:16-22; 4:18-20 ✓
1 Peter 2:13-17

2 **Saturday**
Ezekiel 34:1-16
Luke 15:1-7

Sunday
Acts 2:42-47
Psalm 23
1 Peter 2:19-25
John 10:1-10

Reflection on Sunday
Daily: Psalm 100

4 **Monday**
Ezekiel 34:17-23
1 Peter 5:1-5

5 **Tuesday**
Ezekiel 34:23-31
Hebrews 13:20-21

6 **Wednesday**
Jeremiah 23:1-8
Matthew 20:17-28

The General Rule of Discipleship
To witness to Jesus Christ in the world and to follow his teachings
through acts of compassion, justice, worship, and devotion under the guidance of the Holy Spirit.

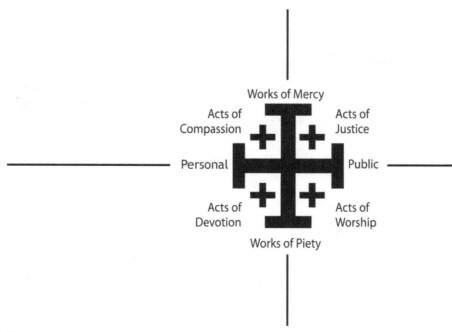

A Word from John Wesley

But when he is born of God, born of the Spirit, how is the manner of his existence changed! His whole soul is now sensible of God, and he can say, by sure experience, "Thou art about my bed, and about my path;" I feel thee in all my ways: "Thou besettest me behind and before, and layest thy hand upon me." The Spirit or breath of God is immediately inspired, breathed into the new-born soul; and the same breath which comes from, returns to, God: As it is continually received by faith, so it is continually rendered back by love, by prayer, and praise, and thanksgiving; love and praise, and prayer being the breath of every soul which is truly born of God.

Sermon 19: The Great Privilege of Those That Are Born of God, §I.8

A Hymn from Charles Wesley

Thou the good Shepherd art,
From thee I ne'er shall part:
Thou my keeper and my guide,
Make me still thy tender care;
Gently lead me by thy side,
Sweetly in thy bosom bear.

Thou art my daily bread;
O Christ, thou art my head!
Motion, virtue, strength to me,
Me, thy living member, flow;
Nourished I, and fed by thee,
Up to thee in all things grow.

(*Collection*-1781, #186:4 & 5; 66.77.77)

Prayers, Comments & Questions

Holy Shepherd, you know your sheep by name and lead us to safety through the valleys of death. Guide us by your voice, that we may walk in certainty and security to the joyous feast prepared in your house, where we celebrate with you forever. Amen.

May

Fifth Sunday of Easter

10

Preparation for Sunday
Psalm 31:1-5, 15-16

Thursday
Genesis 12:1-3
Acts 6:8-15

Friday
Exodus 3:1-12
Acts 7:1-16

Saturday
Jeremiah 26:20-24
John 8:48-59

Sunday
Acts 7:55-60
Psalm 31:1-5, 15-16
1 Peter 2:2-10
John 14:1-14

Reflection on Sunday
Daily: Psalm 102:1-17

Monday
Exodus 13:17-22
Acts 7:17-40

Tuesday
Proverbs 3:5-12
Acts 7:44-56

Wednesday
Proverbs 3:13-18
John 8:31-38

The General Rule of Discipleship
To witness to Jesus Christ in the world and to follow his teachings
through acts of compassion, justice, worship, and devotion under the guidance of the Holy Spirit.

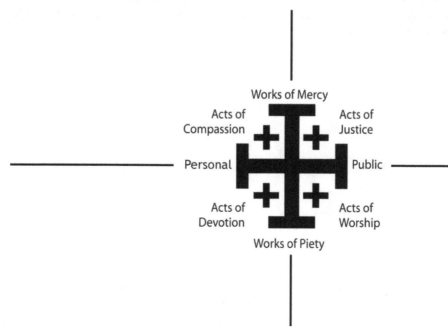

A Word from John Wesley

And being taught of Christ who was meek as well as lowly in heart, we shall then be enabled to "walk with all meekness;" being taught of Him who teacheth as never man taught, to be meek as well as lowly in heart. This implies not only a power over anger, but over all violent and turbulent passions. It implies the having all our passions in due proportion; none of them either too strong or too weak; but all duly balanced with each other; all subordinate to reason; and reason directed by the Spirit of God.

Sermon 74-"On The Church", ¶ 24

A Hymn from Charles Wesley

Jesu, show us thy salvation,
(In thy strength we strive with thee)
By thy mystic incarnation,
By thy pure nativity,
Save us thou, our New-Creator,
Into all our souls impart,
Thy divine un-sinning nature,
Form thyself within our heart.

From the world of care release us,
By thy decent burial save,
Crucified with thee, O Jesus,
Hide us in thy quiet grave:
By thy power divinely glorious,
By thy resurrection's power
Raise us up, o'er sin victorious,
Raise us up to fall no more.

(*Hymns for Our Lord's Resurrection*—1746, #7:1 & 6; 87.87.87.87)

Prayers, Comments & Questions

Risen Christ, you prepare a place for us, in the home of the Mother-and-Father of us all. Draw us more deeply into yourself, through scripture read, water splashed, bread broken, wine poured, so that when our hearts are troubled, we will know you more completely as the way, the truth, and the life. Amen.

May

Sixth Sunday of Easter

Preparation for Sunday
Daily: Psalm 66:8-20

Thursday
Genesis 6:5-22
Acts 27:1-12

Friday
Genesis 7:1-24
Acts 27:13-38

Saturday
Genesis 8:13-19
John 14:27-29

Sunday
Acts 17:22-31
Psalm 66:8-20
1 Peter 3:13-22
John 14:15-21

Reflection on Sunday
Daily: Psalm 93

Monday
Genesis 9:8-17
Acts 27:39-44

Tuesday
Deuteronomy 5:22-33
1 Peter 3:8-12

Wednesday
Deuteronomy 31:1-13
John 16:16-24

The General Rule of Discipleship
*To witness to Jesus Christ in the world and to follow his teachings
through acts of compassion, justice, worship, and devotion under the guidance of the Holy Spirit.*

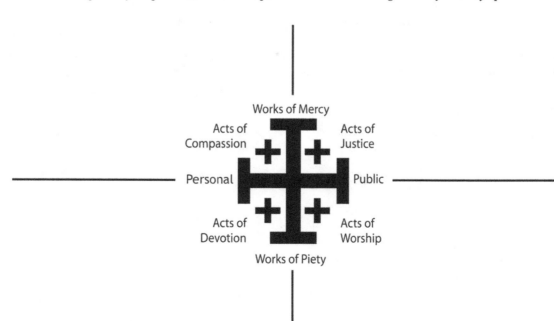

A Word from John Wesley

Walk with all " longsuffering." This is nearly related to meekness, but implies something more. It carries on the victory already gained over all your turbulent passions; notwithstanding all the powers of darkness, all the assaults of evil men or evil spirits. It is patiently triumphant over all opposition, and unmoved though all the waves and storms thereof go over you. Though provoked ever so often, it is still the same, quiet and unshaken; never being "overcome of evil," but overcoming evil with good.

Sermon 74-"On The Church", ¶ 25

A Hymn from Charles Wesley

O that the Comforter would come!
Nor visit as a transient guest,
But fix in me his constant home,
And take possession of my breast;
And fix in me his loved abode,
The temple of indwelling God!

Come, Holy Ghost, my heart inspire!
Attest that I am born again!
Come, and baptize me now with fire,
Nor let thy former gifts be vain.
I cannot rest in sins forgiven;
Where is the earnest of my heaven?

(*Collection*-1781, #365:3 & 4; 88.88.88)

Prayers, Comments & Questions

Living and gracious God, through the death and resurrection of Jesus you have brought us out to a spacious place where we are called to live as those redeemed. Empower us by your Spirit to keep your commandments, that we may show forth your love with gentle word and reverent deed to all your people. Amen.

May

Seventh Sunday of Easter

24

Thursday
Ascension of the Lord
Acts 1:1-11
Psalm 47 *or* Psalm 93
Ephesians 1:15-23
Luke 24:44-53

21 **Preparation for Sunday**
Daily: Psalm 93

Friday
22
2 Kings 2:1-12
Ephesians 2:1-7

23 ### Saturday
2 Kings 2:13-15
John 8:21-30

Sunday
Acts 1:6-14
Psalm 68:1-10, 32-35
1 Peter 4:12-14; 5:6-11
John 17:1-11

25

Reflection on Sunday
Daily: Psalm 99

Monday
Leviticus 9:1-11, 22-24
1 Peter 4:1-6

26 ### Tuesday
Numbers 16:41-50
1 Peter 4:7-11

27 ### Wednesday
1 Kings 8:54-65
John 3:31-36

The General Rule of Discipleship
To witness to Jesus Christ in the world and to follow his teachings
through acts of compassion, justice, worship, and devotion under the guidance of the Holy Spirit.

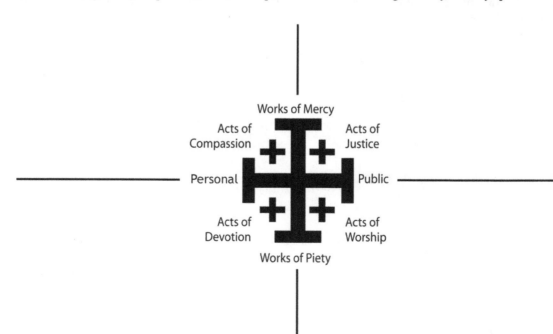

A Word from John Wesley

The "forbearing one another in love" seems to mean, not only the not resenting anything, and the not avenging yourselves; not only the not injuring, hurting, or grieving each other, either by word or deed; but also the bearing one another's burdens; yea, and lessening them by every means in our power. It implies the sympathizing with them in their sorrows, afflictions, and infirmities; the bearing them up when, without our help, they would be liable to sink under their burdens; the endeavouring to lift their sinking heads, and to strengthen their feeble knees.

Sermon 74-"On The Church", ¶ 26

A Hymn from Charles Wesley

By the pomp of thine ascending,
Live we here to heaven restored,
Live in pleasures never ending,
Share the portion of our Lord:
Let us have our conversation
With the blessed Spirits above,
Saved with all thy great salvation,
Perfectly renewed in Love.

Glorious Head, triumphant Saviour,
High enthroned above all height,
We have now through thee found favour,
Righteous in thy Father's sight:
Hears he not thy prayer unceasing?
Can he turn away thy face:
Send us down the purchased blessing,
Fulness of the gospel-grace.

(*Hymns for Our Lord's Resurrection*—1746, #7:7 & 8; 87.87.87.87)

Prayers, Comments & Questions

Ascension of the Lord
Precious Love, your ascended Son promised the gift of holy power. Send your Spirit of revelation and wisdom, that in the blessed freedom of hope, we may witness to the grace of forgiveness and sing songs of joy with the peoples of earth to the One who makes us one body. Amen.

Seventh Sunday of Easter
O God of glory, your Son Jesus Christ suffered for us and ascended to your right hand. Unite us with Christ and each other in suffering and in joy, that all your children may be drawn into your bountiful dwelling. Amen.

Day of Pentecost

Preparation for Sunday
Daily: Psalm 33:12-22

28 **Thursday**
Exodus 19:1-9a
Acts 2:1-11

29 **Friday**
Exodus 19:16-25
Romans 8:14-17

30 **Saturday**
Exodus 20:1-21
Matthew 5:1-12

34 **Sunday**
Acts 2:1-21
or Numbers 11:24-30
Psalm 104:24-34, 35b
1 Corinthians 12:3b-13
or Acts 2:1-21
John 20:19-23
or John 7:37-39

June

Reflection on Sunday
Daily: Psalm 104:24-34, 35b

1 **Monday**
Joel 2:18-29
Romans 8:18-24

2 **Tuesday**
Ezekiel 39:7-8, 21-29
Romans 8:26-27

3 **Wednesday**
Numbers 11:24-30
John 7:37-39

The General Rule of Discipleship

To witness to Jesus Christ in the world and to follow his teachings
through acts of compassion, justice, worship, and devotion under the guidance of the Holy Spirit.

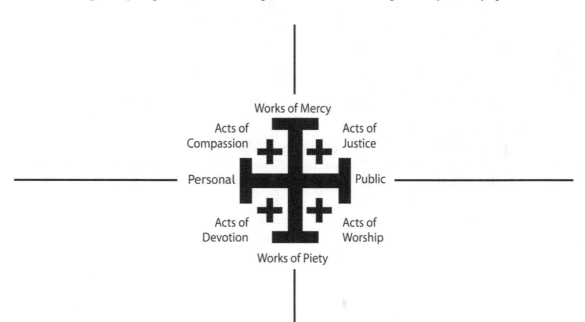

A Word from John Wesley

The true members of the Church of Christ "endeavour," with all possible diligence, with all care and pains, with unwearied patience, (and all will be little enough,) to "keep the unity of the Spirit in the bond of peace;" to preserve inviolate the same spirit of lowliness and meekness, of longsuffering, mutual forbearance, and love; and all these cemented and knit together by that sacred tie, the peace of God filling the heart. Thus only can we be and continue living members of that Church which is the body of Christ.

Sermon 74-"On The Church", ¶ 27

A Hymn from Charles Wesley

Sinners, lift up your hearts,
The promise to receive!
Jesus himself imparts,
He comes in man to live;
The Holy Ghost to man is given;
Rejoice in God sent down from heaven.

Jesus is Glorified,
And gives the Comforter,
His Spirit to reside
In all his members here:
The Holy Ghost to man is given;
Rejoice in God sent down from heaven.

(*Hymns for Whitsunday*—1746, #4:1 & 2; 66.66.88)

Prayers, Comments & Questions

Perplexing, Pentecostal God, you infuse us with your Spirit, urging us to vision and dream. May the gift of your presence find voice in our lives, that our babbling may be transformed into discernment and the flickering of many tongues light an unquenchable fire of compassion and justice. Amen.

Season after Pentecost

Disciples in Ministry in Christ's Name and the Spirit's Power

This season is sometimes also referred to as "Ordinary Time," but it is intended to be far from "ordinary" in terms of its purposes in supporting and strengthening your discipleship to Jesus Christ. The word *Ordinary* here actually only refers to the "ordinal numbers" (first, second, third, and so on) used to refer to which Sunday after Pentecost a given Sunday may be through this season.

Rather than ordinary or "ho-hum," the idea of this season is to support disciples and the whole congregation in living out the gifts and callings discerned during Easter Season and commissioned on the Day of Pentecost. In the Northern Hemisphere, this season typically corresponds with "summer," when schools are out, and wide varieties of vacation schedules may mean the ability to coordinate or even operate some ministries in the congregation (such as Sunday School or some choirs) may be challenged or curtailed until a relaunch in the fall. This scheduling situation makes it even more critical for congregations and individuals to make sure the profound formational and missional purposes of this season are not overlooked, but intentionally planned for.

If you are using *A Disciple's Journal*, chances are you are already intent on strengthening your own discipleship. Let me encourage you to take another step. Ask your pastor to work with you to gather others who will take these months as an intentional journey of accountable discipleship and growth in ministry with you. Your congregation may not be able to provide a "program" for everyone who does this, but your pastor can certainly help you gather a "coalition of the willing" who will.

As you do, keep in mind that with the exceptions of Trinity Sunday and Christ the King Sunday, which begin and end this season, and All Saints, which falls during it, the three major tracks of readings (Old Testament, Epistle, and Gospel) are all "semi-continuous" during this season. None is intended to relate to the other, except for the "Bookend Sundays" and All Saints. The Old Testament readings are selections from the stories of the prophets, kings and patriarchs/matriarchs (depending on the year). The Epistle readings explore the meaning and practice of the Christian life, in particular early Christian communities. And the Gospel readings take us on a journey through the ministry and teaching of Jesus.

As suggested for the Season after Epiphany, you may wish to coordinate the way you and your group focus your energy and attention on the daily readings through these months with the particular stream of texts your congregation's worship leaders focus on during this time as a means to help reinforce the themes of the Sunday readings with your daily discipleship and ministry through these months.

Rev. Taylor Burton-Edwards

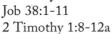

Trinity Sunday

Preparation for Sunday
Daily: Psalm 8

 Thursday
Job 38:1-11
2 Timothy 1:8-12a

Friday
Job 38:12-21
2 Timothy 1:12b-14

Saturday
Job 38:22-38
John 14:15-17

Sunday
Genesis 1:1—2:4a
Psalm 8
2 Corinthians 13:11-13
Matthew 28:16-20

Reflection on Sunday
Daily: Psalm 29

Monday
Job 38:39—39:12
1 Corinthians 12:1-3

Tuesday
Job 39:13-25
1 Corinthians 12:4-13

Wednesday
Job 39:26—40:5
John 14:25-26

The General Rule of Discipleship
To witness to Jesus Christ in the world and to follow his teachings
through acts of compassion, justice, worship, and devotion under the guidance of the Holy Spirit.

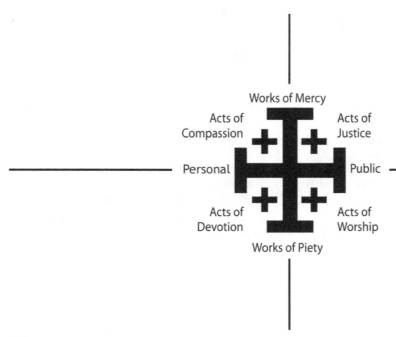

A Word from John Wesley

What is then the perfection of which man is capable while he dwells in a corruptible body? It is the complying with that kind command, "My son, give me thy heart." It is the "loving the Lord his God with all his heart, and with all his soul and with all his mind." This is the sum of Christian perfection: It is all comprised in that one word, Love. The first branch of it is the love of God: And as he that loves God loves his brother also, it is inseparably connected with the second: "Thou shalt love thy neighbour as thyself:" Thou shalt love every man as thy own soul, as Christ loved us. "On these two commandments hang all the Law and the Prophets:" These contain the whole of Christian perfection.

Sermon 76: On Perfection, § I.4

A Hymn from Charles Wesley

Our heavenly Father is but One
With that Paternity
In which the Father and the Son
And Holy Ghost agree:
Each Person of the Triune God,
May his own creature claim,
For each impressed the earthly clod
With his own awful Name.

Father, and Son, and Spirit joined
In the creating plan,
Each is the Maker of mankind,
And doth his work sustain:
The Spirit breathed his life into
Our animated clay,
And he begets our souls anew,
And seals us to that day.

To Father, Son, and Holy Ghost
We equal homage pay,
And each in whom we wholly trust,
Implicitly obey:
Ourselves entirely we resign
To the great Three in One,
And worship properly divine
Perform to God alone.

(*Hymns on the Trinity*—1767, #39:1, 2 & 5; 86.86.86.86)

Prayers, Comments & Questions

God, our Father, whose fingers sculpt sun and moon and curl the baby's ear; Spirit, brooding over chaos before the naming of day; Savior, sending us to earth's ends with water and words: startle us with the grace, love, and communion of your unity in diversity, that we may live to the praise of your majestic name. Amen.

Sunday between May 24 and 28 inclusive
if after Trinity Sunday

Preparation for Sunday
Daily: Psalm 131

Thursday
Proverbs 12:22-28
Philippians 2:19-24

Friday
Isaiah 26:1-6
Philippians 2:25-30

Saturday
Isaiah 31:1-9
Luke 11:14-23

Sunday
Isaiah 49:8-16a
Psalm 131
1 Corinthians 4:1-5
Matthew 6:24-34

Reflection on Sunday
Daily: Psalm 104

Monday
Deuteronomy 32:1-14
Hebrews 10:32-39

Tuesday
1 Kings 17:1-16
1 Corinthians 4:6-21

Wednesday
Isaiah 66:7-13
Luke 12:22-31

The General Rule of Discipleship
To witness to Jesus Christ in the world and to follow his teachings
through acts of compassion, justice, worship, and devotion under the guidance of the Holy Spirit.

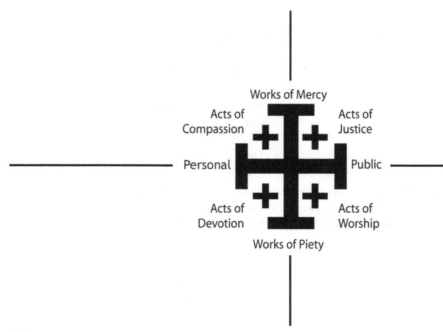

A Word from John Wesley

Another view of this is given us in those words of the great Apostle: "Let this mind be in you which was also in Christ Jesus." For although this immediately and directly refers to the humility of our Lord, yet it may be taken in a far more extensive sense, so as to include the whole disposition of his mind, all his affections, all his tempers, both toward God and man. Now, it is certain that as there was no evil affection in him, so no good affection or temper was wanting. So that "whatsoever things are holy, whatsoever things are lovely," are all included in "the mind that was in Christ Jesus."

Sermon 76: On Perfection, § I.5

A Hymn from Charles Wesley

Our heavenly Master is but One,
And Jesus is his name:
But Jesus the eternal Son
Is with his Sire the same:
The Spirit's glorious plenitude
Resides in Christ adored:
Each Person doth the Three include,
And each we call our Lord.

Taught by our Father in the skies,
Taught by our Saviour there,
Taught by the Holy Ghost, and wise
We to salvation are:
Our God is One in Persons Three,
Our Teacher is but One,
Who calls us up with joy to see
Jehovah on his throne.

(*Hymns on the Trinity*—1767, 40, 86.86.86.86)

Prayers, Comments & Questions

Grant, O Lord, that the course of this world may be peaceably governed by your providence; and that your Church may joyfully serve you in confidence and serenity; through Jesus Christ our Lord, who lives and reigns with you and the Holy Spirit, one God, for ever and ever. Amen.

Sunday between May 29 and June 4 inclusive
if after Trinity Sunday

Preparation for Sunday
Daily: Psalm 46

Thursday
Genesis 1:1—2:4a
Romans 2:17-29

Friday
Genesis 2:4b-25
Romans 9:6-13

Saturday
Genesis 3:1-24
Matthew 7:1-6

Sunday
Genesis 6:9-22; 7:24;
    8:14-19
Psalm 46
Romans 1:16-17; 3:22b-31
Matthew 7:21-29

Reflection on Sunday
Daily: Psalm 69:1-3, 13-16,
30-36

Monday
Genesis 4:1-16
Romans 2:1-11

Tuesday
Genesis 4:17—5:5
Romans 3:9-22a

Wednesday
Genesis 11:1-9 *Tower of Babel*
Matthew 7:13-20

The General Rule of Discipleship
*To witness to Jesus Christ in the world and to follow his teachings
through acts of compassion, justice, worship, and devotion under the guidance of the Holy Spirit.*

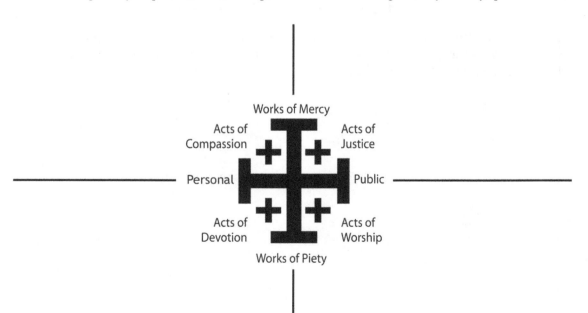

A Word from John Wesley

St. Paul, when writing to the Galatians, places perfection in yet another view. It is the one undivided fruit of the Spirit, which he describes thus: "The fruit of the Spirit is love, joy, peace, longsuffering gentleness, goodness, fidelity," (so the word should be translated here,) "meekness, temperance." What a glorious constellation of graces is here! Now, suppose all these things to be knit together in one, to be united together in the soul of a believer, this is Christian perfection.

Sermon 76: On Perfection, § I.6

A Hymn from Charles Wesley

The only wise almighty God
Is able by his grace
Us to present, in love renewed
Before his glorious face:
And he whose promises are sure,
Returning for his bride,
Will to himself present us pure,
And wholly sanctified.

Jesus, who bought us with his blood,
Who makes us pure in heart.
The only wise, almighty God,
Our Saviour we assert:
The glorious presence is his own;
And when the sight is given,
Beholding Jesus on his throne,
We reach our highest heaven.

(*Hymns on the Trinity*—1767, 47, 86.86.86.86)

Prayers, Comments & Questions

God With Us, whose unfailing mercy is our refuge even when our broken choices corrupt your glorious creation: lead us to the safe haven of righteousness and uphold us on the rock of your presence, so that in times of trial we may stand firm, anchored in faith, through Christ, our rock and our redeemer. Amen.

Sunday between June 5 and 11 inclusive
if after Trinity Sunday

Preparation for Sunday
Daily: Psalm 33:1-12

Thursday
Genesis 13:1-18
2 Peter 2:17-22

Friday
Genesis 14:17-24
Acts 28:1-10

Saturday
Genesis 15:1-20
Matthew 9:27-34

Sunday
Genesis 12:1-9
Psalm 33:1-12
Romans 4:13-25
Matthew 9:9-13, 18-26

Reflection on Sunday
Daily: Psalm 119:41-48

Monday   *Ishmael born*
Genesis 16:1-15
2 Corinthians 6:14—7:2

Tuesday   *now Abraham*
                     covenant
Genesis 17:1-27   *Isaac born*
Hebrews 13:1-16

Wednesday
Genesis 18:16-33
Matthew 12:1-8

The General Rule of Discipleship
To witness to Jesus Christ in the world and to follow his teachings
through acts of compassion, justice, worship, and devotion under the guidance of the Holy Spirit.

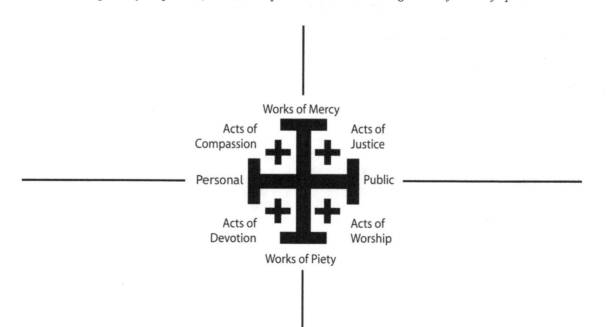

A Word from John Wesley

St. Peter expresses it in a still different manner, though to the same effect: "As he that hath called you is holy, so be ye holy in all manner of conversation." (1 Peter i. 15.) According to this Apostle, then, perfection is another name for universal holiness: Inward and outward righteousness: Holiness of life, arising from holiness of heart.

Sermon 76: On Perfection, § I.8

A Hymn from Charles Wesley

Father, Son, and Spirit, hear
Thy apostate creature's grown,
Languishing to find thee near,
Worshipping a God unknown,
Light 'till in thy light I see,
Know eternal Life in thee.

Creeds and books can nothing do,
Unaccompanied by grace;
Grace must form my soul anew,
Give me to discern thy face,
Bring my faithful heart the power
God in persons three t'adore.

(*Hymns on the Trinity*—1767, p. 92, 6:1 & 2 77.77.77)

Prayers, Comments & Questions

Beckoning God, you promise long journeys and new names. Call us out to risk holy adventure with unusual table companions. Linger with us so that we may be faithful disciples, touching the fringe of your healing on behalf of all your children. Amen.

Sunday between June 12 and 18 inclusive
if after Trinity Sunday

Preparation for Sunday
Daily: Psalm 116:1-2, 12-19

Thursday
Genesis 21:1-7
Hebrews 3:1-6

Friday
Genesis 24:1-9
Acts 7:35-43

Saturday
Genesis 24:10-52
Mark 7:1-13

Sunday
Genesis 18:1-15, 21:1-7
Psalm 116:1-2, 12-19
Romans 5:1-8
Matthew 9:35—10:23

Reflection on Sunday
Daily: Psalm 126

Monday
Genesis 23:1-19
1 Thessalonians 3:1-5

Tuesday
Genesis 25:7-11
2 Thessalonians 2:13—3:5

Wednesday
Nehemiah 9:1-8
Luke 6:12-19

The General Rule of Discipleship
To witness to Jesus Christ in the world and to follow his teachings
through acts of compassion, justice, worship, and devotion under the guidance of the Holy Spirit.

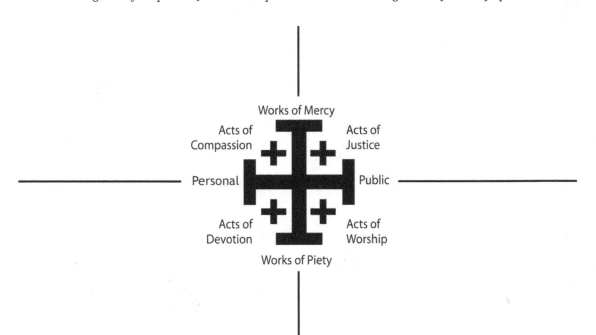

A Word from John Wesley

Notwithstanding a spark of knowledge glimmering here and there, the whole earth was covered with darkness, till the Sun of righteousness arose and scattered the shades of night. Since this day-spring from on high has appeared, a great light hath shined unto those who, till then, sat in darkness and in the shadow of death. And thousands of them in every age have known, "that God so loved the world, as to give his only Son, to the end that whosoever believeth on him should not perish, but have everlasting life." And being entrusted with the oracles of God, they have known that God hath also given us his Holy Spirit, who "worketh in us both to will and to do of his good pleasure."

Sermon 85: On Working Out Our Own Salvation, ¶ 3

A Hymn from Charles Wesley

But thou drawst me after thee,
But thou dost my heart incline,
Helping its infirmity
Now to ask the grace divine:
Now this unbelief remove,
Tell me now that thou art Love.

Father, manifest thy Son,
Son, to me the Father show,
Holy Comforter, make known
The deep things of God below,
Sovereign, Triune God, impart
All thy fulness to my heart.

(*Hymns on the Trinity*—1767, p. 92, 6:3 & 4, 77.77.77)

Prayers, Comments & Questions

God of the prophets and apostles, you greeted old Abraham and Sarah with news of wonder and life. Send us into the world to preach good news, as Jesus did, heal the sick, resist evil, and bring the outcast home. Amen.

Sunday between June 19 and 25 inclusive

if after Trinity Sunday

Preparation for Sunday
Daily: Psalm 86:1-10

21

Sunday *Hagar & Ishmael sent away*
Genesis 21:8-21
Psalm 86:1-10, 16-17
Romans 6:1b-11
Matthew 10:24-39

Reflection on Sunday
Daily: Psalm 86:11-17

18

Thursday
Exodus 12:43-49
Hebrews 2:5-9

22 **Monday** *Ishmael born*
Genesis 16:1-15
Revelation 2:1-7

19

Friday
Genesis 35:1-4
Acts 5:17-26

23 **Tuesday**
Genesis 25:12-18
Revelation 2:8-11

20

Saturday
Ezekiel 29:3-7
Luke 11:53—12:3

24 **Wednesday**
Jeremiah 42:18-22
Matthew 10:5-23

The General Rule of Discipleship
To witness to Jesus Christ in the world and to follow his teachings
through acts of compassion, justice, worship, and devotion under the guidance of the Holy Spirit.

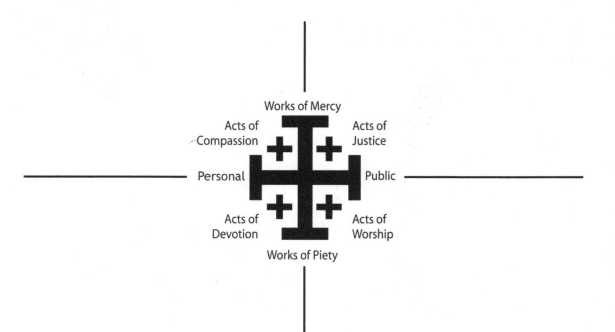

A Word from John Wesley

Salvation begins with what is usually termed (and very properly) preventing grace; including the first wish to please God, the first dawn of light concerning his will, and the first slight transient conviction of having sinned against him. All these imply some tendency toward life; some degree of salvation; the beginning of a deliverance from a blind, unfeeling heart, quite insensible of God and the things of God.

Sermon 85: On Working Out Our Own Salvation, § II.1

A Hymn from Charles Wesley

O for a heart to praise my God,
A heart from sin set free!
A heart that always feels thy blood,
So freely spilt for me!

A heart resigned, submissive, meek,
My great Redeemer's throne,
Where only Christ is heard to speak,
Where Jesus reigns alone.

(*Collection*-1781, #334:1 & 2; CM)

Prayers, Comments & Questions

God of strength and courage, in Jesus Christ you set us free from sin and death, and call us to the risk of faith and service. Give us grace to follow him who gave himself for others, that, by our service, we may find the life he came to bring. Amen.

Sunday between June 26 and July 2 inclusive

Preparation for Sunday
Daily: Psalm 13

25 Thursday
Micah 7:18-20
Galatians 5:2-6

26 Friday
2 Chronicles 20:5-12
Galatians 5:7-12

27 Saturday
Genesis 26:23-25
Luke 17:1-4

28 Sunday
Genesis 22:1-14
Psalm 13
Romans 6:12-23
Matthew 10:40-42

Reflection on Sunday
Daily: Psalm 47

29 Monday
Genesis 22:15-18
1 Thessalonians 4:9-12

30 Tuesday
1 Kings 18:36-39
1 John 4:1-6

Wednesday
Isaiah 51:1-3
Matthew 11:20-24

The General Rule of Discipleship
*To witness to Jesus Christ in the world and to follow his teachings
through acts of compassion, justice, worship, and devotion under the guidance of the Holy Spirit.*

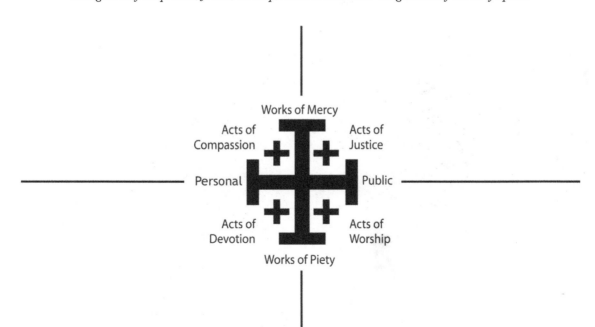

A Word from John Wesley

Salvation is carried on by convincing grace, usually in Scripture termed repentance; which brings a larger measure of self-knowledge, and a farther deliverance from the heart of stone. Afterwards we experience the proper Christian salvation; whereby, "through grace," we "are saved by faith;" consisting of those two grand branches, justification and sanctification.

Sermon 85: On Working Out Our Own Salvation, § II.1

A Hymn from Charles Wesley

O for a lowly, contrite heart,
Believing, true, and clean,
Which neither life nor death can part
From him that dwells within!

A heart in every thought renewed,
And full of love divine,
Perfect, and right, and pure, and good—
A copy, Lord, of thine!

(*Collection*-1781, #334:3 & 4; CM)

Prayers, Comments & Questions

Ruler of the universe, you call us to radical loyalty beyond all earthly claim. Grant us strength to offer ourselves to you as people who have been raised from death to life through Jesus Christ, who lives and reigns with you and the Holy Spirit, one God, now and for ever. Amen.

Sunday between July 3 and 9 inclusive

Preparation for Sunday
Daily: Psalm 45:10-17

Thursday
Genesis 25:19-27
Romans 7:1-6

Friday
Genesis 27:1-17
Romans 7:7-20

Saturday
Genesis 27:18-29
Luke 10:21-24

Sunday
Genesis 24:34-38,
42-49, 58-67
Psalm 45:10-17
Romans 7:15-25a
Matthew 11:16-19, 25-30

Reflection on Sunday
Daily: Song of Solomon 2:8-13

Monday
Genesis 27:30-46
Romans 1:18-25

Tuesday
Genesis 29:1-14
Romans 3:1-8

Wednesday
Genesis 29:31-35
John 13:1-17

The General Rule of Discipleship
*To witness to Jesus Christ in the world and to follow his teachings
through acts of compassion, justice, worship, and devotion under the guidance of the Holy Spirit.*

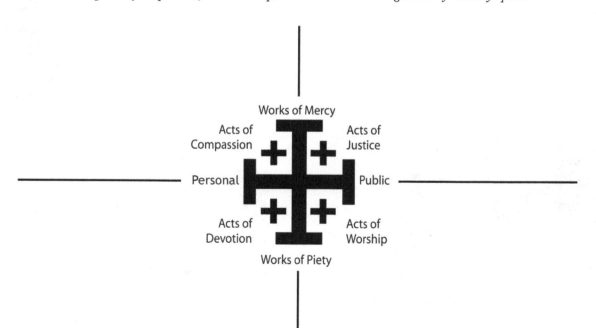

A Word from John Wesley

By justification we are saved from the guilt of sin, and restored to the favour of God; by sanctification we are saved from the power and root of sin, and restored to the image of God. All experience, as well as Scripture, show this salvation to be both instantaneous and gradual. It begins the moment we are justified, in the holy, humble, gentle, patient love of God and man. It gradually increases from that moment, as "a grain of mustard seed, which, at first, is the least of all seeds," but afterwards puts forth large branches, and becomes a great tree; till, in another instant, the heart is cleansed from all sin, and filled with pure love to God and man. But even that love increases more and more, till we "grow up in all things into Him that is our Head;" till we attain "the measure of the stature of the fulness of Christ."

Sermon 85: On Working Out Our Own Salvation, § II.1

A Hymn from Charles Wesley

To save what was lost
From heaven he came.
Come, sinners, and trust
In Jesus' name!
He offers you pardon,
He bids you be free!
If sin is your burden,
O come unto me!

O let me commend
My Saviour to you,
The publican's friend,
And advocate too;
For you he is pleading
His merits and death,
With God interceding
For sinners beneath.

(*Collection*-1781, #5:3 & 4; Irregular)

Prayers, Comments & Questions

We give you thanks, O God of compassion, for the salvation you have revealed to the little ones through Christ Jesus, our wisdom and strength. Teach us to take up his gentle yoke and find rest from our burdens and cares. Amen.

Sunday between July 10 and 16 inclusive

Preparation for Sunday
Daily: Psalm 119:105-112

12 **Sunday** *Isaacs sons Escau + Jacob*
Genesis 25:19-34
Psalm 119:105-112
Romans 8:1-11
Matthew 13:1-9, 18-23

Reflection on Sunday
Daily: Psalm 142

9 **Thursday**
Exodus 3:1-6
Romans 2:12-16

10 **Friday**
Deuteronomy 32:1-10
Romans 15:14-21

11 **Saturday**
Isaiah 2:1-4
John 12:44-50

13 **Monday**
Micah 1:1-5
1 Thessalonians 4:1-8

14 **Tuesday**
Jeremiah 49:7-11
Ephesians 4:17—5:2

15 **Wednesday**
Obadiah 15-21
Matthew 13:10-17

The General Rule of Discipleship
To witness to Jesus Christ in the world and to follow his teachings
through acts of compassion, justice, worship, and devotion under the guidance of the Holy Spirit.

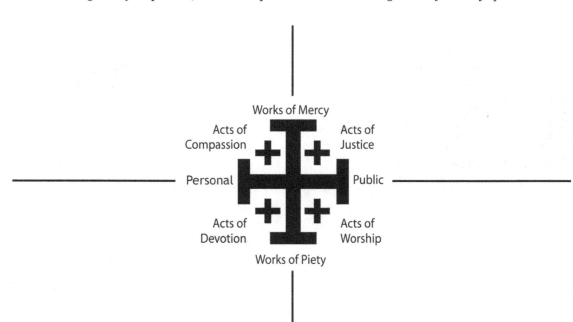

A Word from John Wesley

But what are the steps which the Scriptures direct us to take, in the working out of our own salvation? The Prophet Isaiah gives us a general answer, touching the first steps which we are to take: "Cease to do evil; learn to do well." If ever you desire that God should work in you that faith whereof cometh both present and eternal salvation, by the grace already given fly from all sin as from the face of a serpent; carefully avoid every evil word and work; yea, abstain from all appearance of evil. And "learn to do well:" Be zealous of good works, of works of piety, as well as works of mercy; family prayer, and crying to God in secret.

Sermon 85: On Working Out Our Own Salvation, § II.4

A Hymn from Charles Wesley

While in thy Word we search for thee
(We search with trembling awe!)
Open our eyes, and let us see
The wonders of thy law.

Now let our darkness comprehend
The light that shines so clear;
Now the revealing Spirit send,
And give us ears to hear.

(*Collection*-1781, #86: 2 & 3, CM)

Prayers, Comments & Questions

O God of mercy, in Jesus Christ you freed us from sin and death, and by your Holy Spirit you nourish our mortal bodies with life. Plant us now in good soil, that our lives may flower in righteousness and peace. Amen.

Sunday between July 17 and 23 inclusive

Preparation for Sunday
Daily: Psalm 139:1-12, 23-24

Thursday *(16)*
Isaiah 44:1-5
Hebrews 2:1-9

Friday *(17)*
Ezekiel 39:21-29
Hebrews 6:13-20

Saturday *(18)*
Exodus 14:9-25
Matthew 7:15-20

Sunday *(19)* — *Jacob's dream at Bethel*
Genesis 28:10-19a
Psalm 139:1-12, 23-24
Romans 8:12-25
Matthew 13:24-30, 36-43

Reflection on Sunday
Daily: Psalm 139:13-18

Monday *(20)* — *Jacob reconcile with Esau*
Genesis 32:3-21
Revelation 14:12-20

Tuesday *(21)* — *Esau forgives Jacob*
Genesis 33:1-17
Galatians 4:21—5:1

Wednesday *(22)* — *Promised covenant to Jacob!*
Genesis 35:16-29
Matthew 12:15-21

The General Rule of Discipleship
To witness to Jesus Christ in the world and to follow his teachings
through acts of compassion, justice, worship, and devotion under the guidance of the Holy Spirit.

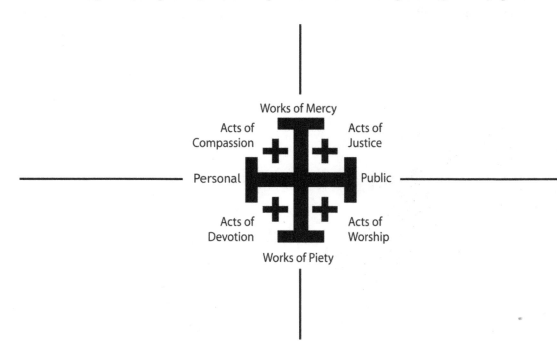

Works of Mercy

Acts of Compassion — Acts of Justice

Personal — Public

Acts of Devotion — Acts of Worship

Works of Piety

A Word from John Wesley

As ye have time, do good unto all men; to their souls and to their bodies. And herein "be ye steadfast, unmovable, always abounding in the work of the Lord." It then only remains, that ye deny yourselves and take up your cross daily. Deny yourselves every pleasure which does not prepare you for taking pleasure in God, and willingly embrace every means of drawing near to God, though it be a cross, though it be grievous to flesh and blood. Thus when you have redemption in the blood of Christ, you will "go on to perfection;" till "walking in the light as he is in the light," you are enabled to testify, that "he is faithful and just," not only to "forgive" your "sins," but to "cleanse" you "from all unrighteousness."

Sermon 85: On Working Out Our Own Salvation, § II.4

A Hymn from Charles Wesley

All power is to our Jesus given;
O'er earth's rebellious sons he reigns;
He mildly rules the hosts of heaven,
And holds the powers of hell in chains.

The enemy his tares hath sown,
But Christ shall shortly root them up;
Shall cast the dire accuser down,
And disappoint his children's hope;

(*Collection*-1781, #271:2 & 5; LM)

Prayers, Comments & Questions

O God of Jacob, you speak in the light of day and in the dark of night when our sleeping is filled with dreams of heaven and earth. May Jacob's vision remind us to be open and watchful, ready to discover your presence in our midst. Amen.

Sunday between July 24 and 30 inclusive

Preparation for Sunday
26 [handwritten]

Daily: Psalm 105:1-11, 45b

Thursday *Jacob meets* [handwritten]
23 [handwritten]
Genesis 29:1-8 *Rachel* [handwritten]
1 Corinthians 4:14-20

Friday *Jacob marries* [handwritten]
24 [handwritten]
Genesis 29:9-14 *both sisters –* [handwritten]
Acts 7:44-53 *Rachel + Leah* [handwritten]

Saturday *Leah unloved but* [handwritten]
25 [handwritten]
Genesis 29:31—30:24 *has 6 children,* [handwritten]
Matthew 12:38-42 *Rachel has 2 ⚊* [handwritten]
Joseph + Benjamin [handwritten]

Sunday
Genesis 29:15-28
Psalm 105:1-11, 45b
Romans 8:26-39
Matthew 13:31-33, 44-52

Reflection on Sunday
Daily: Psalm 65:8-13

Monday *27* [handwritten]
Genesis 30:25-36
James 3:13-18

Tuesday *28* [handwritten]
Genesis 30:37-43
Ephesians 6:10-18

Wednesday *29* [handwritten]
Genesis 46:2—47:12
Mark 4:30-34

The General Rule of Discipleship
To witness to Jesus Christ in the world and to follow his teachings
through acts of compassion, justice, worship, and devotion under the guidance of the Holy Spirit.

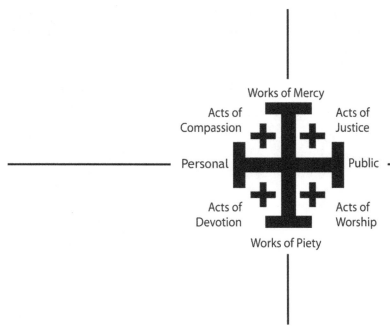

A Word from John Wesley

First, God worketh in you; therefore you can work—otherwise it would be impossible. If he did not work it would be impossible for you to work out your own salvation. 'With man this is impossible', saith our Lord, 'for a rich man to enter into the kingdom of heaven.' Yea, it is impossible for any man; for any that is born of a woman, unless God work in him. Seeing all men are by nature not only sick, but 'dead in trespasses, and sins', it is not possible for them to do anything well till God raises them from the dead. It was impossible for Lazarus to 'come forth' till the Lord had given him life. And it is equally impossible for us to 'come' out of our sins, yea, or to make the least motion toward it, till he who hath all power in heaven and earth calls our dead souls into life.

Sermon 85: On Working Out Our Own Salvation, § III.3

A Hymn from Charles Wesley

Christ, my Master and my Lord,
Let me thy forerunner be;
O be mindful of thy word,
Visit them, and visit me!
To this house, and all herein,
Now let thy salvation come!
Save our souls from inbred sin,
Make us thy eternal home!

Let us never, never rest
Till the promise is fulfilled;
Till we are of thee possessed,
Pardoned, sanctified, and sealed;
Till we all, in love renewed,
Find the pearl that Adam lost,
Temples of the living God,
Father, Son, and Holy Ghost.

(*Collection*-1781, #467:2 & 3; 77.77 D)

Prayers, Comments & Questions

Seed-planting, fish-netting, bread-baking, pearl-hunting God, you shape us into living parables. Pray with you Spirit in us so that we may understand our experiences as healing metaphors, and become creative and abundant stewards of the environment you entrusted to our love. Amen.

Sunday between July 31 and August 6 inclusive

Preparation for Sunday
Daily: Psalm 17:1-7, 15

30 **Thursday**
Isaiah 14:1-2
Philippians 4:10-15

31 **Friday**
Isaiah 41:8-10
Romans 9:6-13

Saturday *Jacob flees with*
Genesis 31:1-21 *family + flock*
Matthew 7:7-11

2 **Sunday** *Jacob wrestles at Peniel with*
Genesis 32:22-31 *"Angel of*
Psalm 17:1-7, 15 *god":*
Romans 9:1-5 *Name*
Matthew 14:13-21 *changed* *3*

from Jacob to Israel

Reflection on Sunday
Daily: Psalm 17:1-7, 15

Monday *Laban overtakes*
Genesis 31:22-42 *Jacob*
Romans 1:8-15

4 **Tuesday** *Jacob appeases*
Genesis 32:3-21 *Esau:*
Acts 2:37-47 *reconciliation*

5 **Wednesday** *Jacob*
Isaiah 43:1-7
Matthew 15:32-39

The General Rule of Discipleship
To witness to Jesus Christ in the world and to follow his teachings
through acts of compassion, justice, worship, and devotion under the guidance of the Holy Spirit.

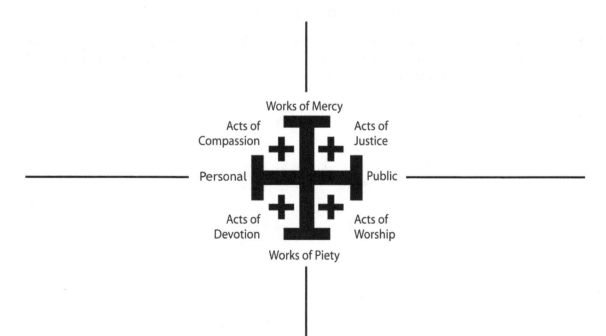

Works of Mercy

Acts of Compassion — Acts of Justice

Personal — Public

Acts of Devotion — Acts of Worship

Works of Piety

A Word from John Wesley

No man living is entirely destitute of what is vulgarly called 'natural conscience'. But this is not natural; it is more properly termed 'preventing grace'. Every man has a greater or less measure of this, which waiteth not for the call of man. Everyone has sooner or later good desires, although the generality of men stifle them before they can strike deep root or produce any considerable fruit. Everyone has some measure of that light, some faint glimmering ray, which sooner or later, more or less, enlightens every man that cometh into the world.

Sermon 85: On Working Out Our Own Salvation, § III.4

A Hymn from Charles Wesley

Give me, Lord, the victory,
My heart's desire fulfil;
Let it now be done to me
According to thy will!
Give me living bread to eat,
And say, in answer to my call,
Canaanite, thy faith is great!
My grace is free for all.

If thy grace for all is free,
Thy call now let me hear;
Show this token upon me,
And bring salvation near.
Now the gracious word repeat,
The word of healing to my soul:
Canaanite, thy faith is great!
Thy faith hath made thee whole..

(*Collection*-1781, #158:5 & 6; 76.76.78.76)

Prayers, Comments & Questions

God beyond all seeing and knowing, we meet you in the night of change and crisis, and wrestle with you in the darkness of doubt. Give us the will and spirit to live faithfully and love as we are loved. Amen.

Sexuality
Old Testament Tu 7pm
sign up

Sunday between August 7 and 13 inclusive

Joseph gets sold by / threw him in pit + but sold to Ismaelts
his brothers.

Preparation for Sunday
Daily: Psalm 105:1-6,
16-22, 45b

Thursday
Genesis 35:22b-29 *Rachel 2 Sons*
Acts 17:10-15 *Leah 10*
Isaac death

6

Friday
Genesis 36:1-8 *Esau 3 wives*
Acts 18:24-28 *moved to Seir*
away from Jacob (Israel) to big
livestock to stay close

7

Saturday
Genesis 37:5-11 *(Israel)*
Matthew 16:1-4 *Jacob seltted in Canaan*
his son Joseph was hated by
brothers

8

Sunday
Genesis 37:1-4, 12-28
Psalm 105:1-6, 16-22, 45b
Romans 10:5-15
Matthew 14:22-33

9

Reflection on Sunday
Daily: Psalm 28
Jacob's coat got torn + returned to father Jacob.

Monday
Genesis 37:29-36
2 Peter 2:4-10 *Jacob "mourning for dead" son*

10

Tuesday
Genesis 39:1-23 *Joseph taken to Egypt*
Romans 9:14-29

11

Wednesday
Genesis 40:1-23 *Joseph able to interpret*
Matthew 8:23-27 *dreams for pharaoh*

12

The General Rule of Discipleship
To witness to Jesus Christ in the world and to follow his teachings
through acts of compassion, justice, worship, and devotion under the guidance of the Holy Spirit.

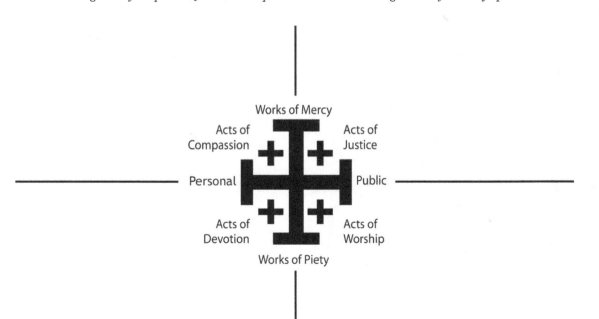

A Word from John Wesley

Inasmuch as God works in you, you are now able to work out your own salvation. Since he worketh in you of his own good pleasure, without any merit of yours, both to will and to do, it is possible for you to fulfil all righteousness. It is possible for you to 'love God, because he hath first loved us', and to 'walk in love', after the pattern of our great Master. We know indeed that word of his to be absolutely true, 'Without me ye can do nothing.' But on the other hand we know, every believer can say, 'I can do all things through Christ that strengtheneth me.'

Sermon 85: On Working Out Our Own Salvation, § III.5

A Hymn from Charles Wesley

Lay thy weighty cross on me,
All my unbelief control;
Till the rebel cease to be
Keep him down within my soul;
That he never more may move,
Root and ground me fast in love.

Give me faith to hold me up,
Walking over life's rough sea;
Holy, purifying hope
Still my soul's sure anchor be;
That I may be always thine,
Perfect me in love divine.

(*Collection*-1781, #176:3 & 4; 77.77.77)

Prayers, Comments & Questions

Through the storms of life, O God, you are with your people in the person of Jesus your Son. Calm our fears and strengthen our faith that we may never doubt his presence among us but proclaim that he is your Son, risen from the dead, living for ever and ever. Amen.

Sunday between August 14 and 20 inclusive

Preparation for Sunday
Daily: Psalm 133

16 **Sunday** *Joseph reveals himself to brothers*
Genesis 45:1-15
Psalm 133
Romans 11:1-2a, 29-32
Matthew 15:10-28

Reflection on Sunday
Daily: Psalm 130

13 **Thursday** *Joseph as prisoner interprets dreams*
Genesis 41:14-36
Revelation 15:1-4

14 **Friday**
Genesis 41:37-57
Acts 14:19-28

Joseph rise to power elevated to rule over pharaoh house

17 **Monday** *Brothers return to Egypt for more grain*
Genesis 43:1-34
Acts 15:1-21

18 **Tuesday** *Joseph detains Benjamin*
Genesis 44:1-34
Romans 11:13-29

15 **Saturday**
Genesis 42:1-28
Matthew 14:34-36

[Jacob (Israel) = father of Joseph] — he sends his sons to Egypt — Jacob has to

19 **Wednesday** *Brothers tell Israel that Joseph is still alive*
Genesis 45:16-28
Matthew 8:1-13

for grain (famine) → move to Egypt. Joseph puts all brothers in prison, until they bring their "youngest" brother back!

The General Rule of Discipleship
To witness to Jesus Christ in the world and to follow his teachings
through acts of compassion, justice, worship, and devotion under the guidance of the Holy Spirit.

Brothers did not know that Joseph knew them as his brothers,

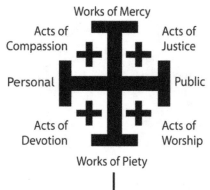

Works of Mercy

Acts of
Compassion

Acts of
Justice

Personal

Public

Acts of
Devotion

Acts of
Worship

Works of Piety

A Word from John Wesley

God worketh in you; therefore you must work: you must be 'workers together with him' (they are the very words of the Apostle); otherwise he will cease working. The general rule on which his gracious dispensations invariably proceed is this: 'Unto him that hath shall be given; but from him that hath not', that does not improve the grace already given, 'shall be taken away what he assuredly hath' (so the words ought to be rendered). Even St. Augustine, who is generally supposed to favour the contrary doctrine, makes that just remark, 'he that made us without ourselves, will not save us without ourselves.'

Sermon 85: On Working Out Our Own Salvation, § III.7

A Hymn from Charles Wesley

Lord, regard my earnest cry,
A potsherd of the earth,
A poor, guilty worm am I,
A Canaanite by birth.
Save me from this tyranny,
From all the power of Satan save;
Mercy, mercy upon me,
Thou Son of David, have!

To the sheep of Israel's fold
Thou in thy flesh wast sent;
Yet the Gentiles now behold
In thee their covenant.
See me then, with pity see,
A sinner whom thou cam'st to save!
Mercy, mercy, upon me,
Thou Son of David, have!

(*Collection*-1781, #158: 1 & 2; 76.76.78.76)

Prayers, Comments & Questions

Holy One of Israel, covenant-keeper, you restore what is lost, heal what is wounded, and gather in those who have been rejected. Give us the faith to speak as steadfastly as did the Canaanite woman, that the outcast may be welcomed and all people may be blessed. Amen.

Sunday between August 21 and 27 inclusive

23

Preparation for Sunday
Daily: Psalm 124

Jacob's last words to his sons

Thursday
Genesis 49:1-33
1 Corinthians 6:1-11

Friday
Genesis 49:29—50:14
2 Corinthians 10:12-18

Jacobs dying wish expresses faith + promise to fulfillment of covenant

Saturday
Genesis 50:15-26
Matthew 16:5-12

Joseph forgives his brothers because it was Jacobs (=father) wish.

Jacob had 12 sons = 12 Tribes of Israel

Sunday
Exodus 1:8—2:10
Psalm 124
Romans 12:1-8
Matthew 16:13-20

Reflection on Sunday
Daily: Psalm 8

Monday
Exodus 1:1-7
Romans 2:1-11

Tuesday
Exodus 2:11-15a
Romans 11:33-36

Wednesday
Exodus 2:15b-22
Matthew 26:6-13

The General Rule of Discipleship
*To witness to Jesus Christ in the world and to follow his teachings
through acts of compassion, justice, worship, and devotion under the guidance of the Holy Spirit.*

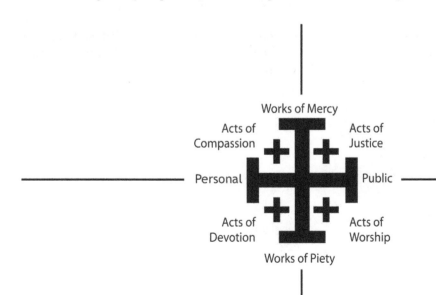

Works of Mercy

Acts of Compassion — Acts of Justice

Personal — Public

Acts of Devotion — Acts of Worship

Works of Piety

A Word from John Wesley

It is generally supposed, that the means of grace, and the ordinances of God, are equivalent terms. We commonly mean by that expression, those that are usually termed, works of piety; viz., hearing and reading the Scripture, receiving the Lord's Supper, public and private prayer, and fasting. And it is certain these are the ordinary channels which convey the grace of God to the souls of men. But are they the only means of grace? Are there no other means than these, whereby God is pleased, frequently, yea, ordinarily, to convey his grace to them that either love or fear him? Surely there are works of mercy, as well as works of piety, which are real means of grace.

Sermon 98: On Visiting the Sick, ¶ 1

A Hymn from Charles Wesley

How happy then are we,
Who build, O Lord, on thee!
What can our foundation shock?
Though the shattered earth remove,
Stands our city on a rock,
On the rock of heavenly love.

A house we call our own,
Which cannot be o'erthrown:
In the general ruin sure,
Storms and earthquakes it defies,
Built immovably secure,
Built eternal in the skies.

(*Collection*-1781, #65:2 & 3; 66.77.77)

Prayers, Comments & Questions

God of Miriam and Moses, you are our help from age to age. Accept our worship, our living sacrifice, and transform us by your Spirit, that, being many members of our true body, we may dare to pray together in the name of Christ our Lord. Amen.

Sunday between August 28 and September 3 inclusive

Preparation for Sunday
Daily: Psalm 105:1-6,
   23-26, 45b

Thursday *27*
Exodus 2:23-24
Ephesians 5:1-6

Friday *28*
Exodus 3:16-25
2 Thessalonians 2:7-12

Saturday *29*
Exodus 4:1-9
Matthew 8:14-17

30 **Sunday**
Exodus 3:1-15
Psalm 105:1-6, 23-26, 45b
Romans 12:9-21
Matthew 16:21-28

Sept

Reflection on Sunday
Daily: Psalm 83:1-4, 13-18

31 **Monday**
Exodus 4:10-31
Revelation 3:1-6

Tuesday *1*
Exodus 5:1—6:13
Revelation 3:7-13

Wednesday *2*
Exodus 7:14-25
Matthew 12:22-32

The General Rule of Discipleship
To witness to Jesus Christ in the world and to follow his teachings
through acts of compassion, justice, worship, and devotion under the guidance of the Holy Spirit.

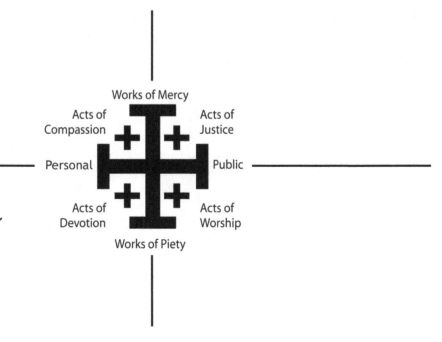

" Bible Hub " for
used info !

A Word from John Wesley

One great reason why the rich, in general, have so little sympathy for the poor, is, because they so seldom visit them. Hence it is, that, according to the common observation, one part of the world does not know what the other suffers. Many of them do not know, because they do not care to know; they keep out of the way of knowing it; and then plead their voluntary ignorance as an excuse for their hardness of heart. "Indeed, Sir," said a person of large substance, "I am a very compassionate man. But, to tell you the truth, I do not know any body in the world that is in want." How did this come to pass? Why, he took good care to keep out of their way; and if he fell upon any of them unawares, "he passed over on the other side."

Sermon 98: On Visiting the Sick, § I.3

A Hymn from Charles Wesley

Pain and sickness, at thy word,
And sin and sorrow flies;
Speak to me, Almighty Lord,
And bid my spirit rise!
Bid me take my burden up,
The bed on which thyself didst lie,
When on Calvary's steep top
My Jesus deigned to die.

Bid me bear the hallowed cross
Which thou hast borne before,
Walk in all thy righteous laws,
And go, and sin no more.
Jesus, I on thee alone
For persevering grace depend!
Love me freely, love thine own,
And love me to the end!

(*Collection*-1781, #160:6 & 7; 76.76.78.76)

Prayers, Comments & Questions

In the flaming bush you promised deliverance to your people, O God, and in the cross of Jesus you embraced our suffering and pain. In times of misery, show us the transforming power of your love that we may know the hope of your glory. Amen.

Sunday between September 4 and 10 inclusive

Preparation for Sunday
Psalm 149

Thursday
Exodus 9:1-7
2 Corinthians 12:11-21

Friday
Exodus 10:21-29
Romans 10:15b-21

Saturday
Exodus 11:1-10
Matthew 23:29-36

Sunday
Exodus 12:1-14
Psalm 149
Romans 13:8-14
Matthew 18:15-20

Reflection on Sunday
Daily: Psalm 121

Monday
Exodus 12:14-28
1 Peter 2:11-17

Tuesday
Exodus 12:29-42
Romans 13:1-7

Wednesday
Exodus 13:1-10
Matthew 21:18-22

The General Rule of Discipleship
*To witness to Jesus Christ in the world and to follow his teachings
through acts of compassion, justice, worship, and devotion under the guidance of the Holy Spirit.*

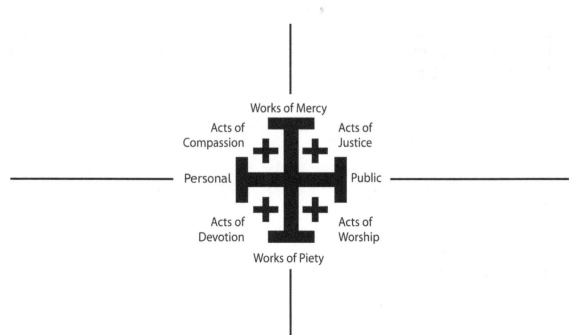

Isaac Romaty

A Word from John Wesley

And first let us inquire, What is *salvation*? The salvation which is here spoken of is not what is frequently understood by that word, the going to heaven, eternal happiness. It is not the soul's going to paradise, termed by our Lord, 'Abraham's bosom'. It is not a blessing which lies on the other side death, or (as we usually speak) in the other world. The very words of the text itself put this beyond all question. 'Ye *are* saved.' It is not something at a distance: it is a present thing, a blessing which, through the free mercy of God, ye are now in possession of. Nay, the words may be rendered, and that with equal propriety, 'Ye *have been* saved.' So that the salvation which is here spoken of might be extended to the entire work of God, from the first dawning of grace in the soul till it is consummated in glory.

Sermon 43: The Scripture Way of Salvation, § I.1

A Hymn from Charles Wesley

Eternal Wisdom, thee we praise,
Thee the creation sings;
With thy loud name, rocks, hills, and seas,
And heaven's high palace rings.

Thy hand, how wide it spreads the sky!
How glorious to behold!
Tinged with a blue of heavenly dye,
And starred with sparkling gold.

There thou hast bid the globes of light
Their endless circles run;
There the pale planet rules the night,
The day obeys the sun.

If down I turn my wond'ring eyes
On clouds and storms below,
Those under-regions of the skies
Thy num'rous glories show.

(*Collection*-1781, #217: 1-4; CM)

Prayers, Comments & Questions

Holy God, you call us to righteousness and light. Teach us the undivided law of love, that we may love your children even as you do, love you with all our will and strength, and find our freedom in this blessed service, taught to us in word and deed by Jesus Christ our Lord. Amen.

Sunday between September 11 and 17 inclusive

Preparation for Sunday
Daily: Psalm 114

Thursday
Exodus 13:17-22
1 John 3:11-16

Friday
Exodus 14:1-18
Acts 7:9-16

Saturday
Exodus 15:19-21
Matthew 6:7-15

Sunday
Exodus 14:19-31
Psalm 114
Romans 14:1-12
Matthew 18:21-35

Reflection on Sunday
Daily: Psalm 77

Monday
Joshua 3:1-17
Hebrews 11:23-29

Tuesday
Nehemiah 9:9-15
Romans 14:13—15:2

Wednesday
2 Kings 2:1-18
Mark 11:20-25

The General Rule of Discipleship
To witness to Jesus Christ in the world and to follow his teachings
through acts of compassion, justice, worship, and devotion under the guidance of the Holy Spirit.

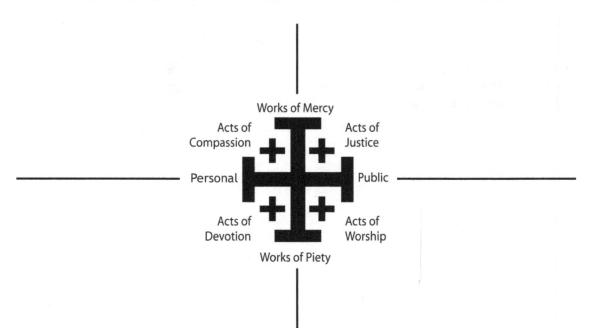

A Word from John Wesley

Justification is another word for pardon. It is the forgiveness of all our sins, and (what is necessarily implied therein) our acceptance with God. The price whereby this hath been procured for us (commonly termed the 'meritorious cause' of our justification) is the blood and righteousness of Christ. or (to express it a little more clearly) all that Christ hath done and suffered for us, till 'he poured out his soul for the transgressors.' The immediate effects of justification are, the peace of God, a 'peace that passeth all understanding', and a 'rejoicing in *hope* of the glory of God', 'with *joy* unspeakable and full of glory'.

Sermon 43: The Scripture Way of Salvation, § I.3

A Hymn from Charles Wesley

The noisy winds stand ready there
Thy orders to obey;
With sounding wings they sweep the air
To make thy chariot way.

There like a trumpet, loud and strong,
Thy thunder shakes our coast;
While the red lightnings wave along
The banners of thy host.

On the thin air, without a prop,
Hang fruitful showers around;
At thy command they sink, and drop
Their fatness on the ground.

Lo! here thy wondrous skill arrays
The earth in cheerful green;
A thousand herbs thy art displays,
A thousand flowers between.

(*Collection*-1781, #217:5-8; CM)

Prayers, Comments & Questions

God of freedom, you brought your people out of slavery with a mighty hand. Deliver us from our captivity to pride and indifference to the needs and gifts of others, that we may be ready to love as you have loved us, and to give even as we have received. Amen.

Sunday between September 18 and 24 inclusive

Preparation for Sunday
Daily: Psalm 105:1-6, 37-45

Thursday
Exodus 15:22-27
2 Corinthians 13:1-4

Friday
Exodus 16:1-21
2 Corinthians 13:5-10

Saturday
Exodus 16:22-30
Matthew 19:23-30

Sunday
Exodus 16:2-15
Psalm 105:1-6, 37-45
Philippians 1:21-30
Matthew 20:1-16

Reflection on Sunday
Daily: Psalm 119:97-104

Monday
Exodus 16:31-35
Romans 16:1-16

Tuesday
Numbers 11:1-9
Romans 16:17-20

Wednesday
Numbers 11:18-23, 31-32
Matthew 18:1-5

The General Rule of Discipleship
*To witness to Jesus Christ in the world and to follow his teachings
through acts of compassion, justice, worship, and devotion under the guidance of the Holy Spirit.*

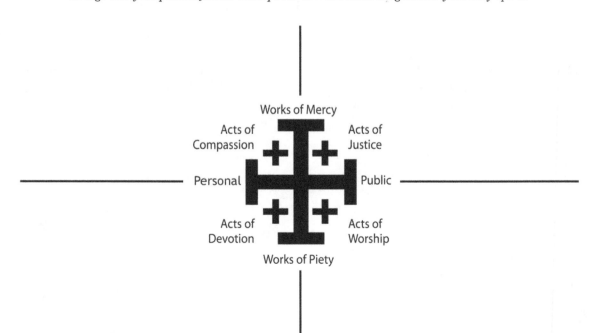

A Word from John Wesley

And at the same time that we are justified, yea, in that very moment, *sanctification* begins. In that instant we are 'born again', 'born from above', 'born of the Spirit'. There is a *real* as well as a *relative* change. We are inwardly renewed by the power of God. We feel the 'love of God shed abroad in our heart by the Holy Ghost which is given unto us', producing love to all mankind, and more especially to the children of God; expelling the love of the world, the love of pleasure, of ease, of honour, of money; together with pride, anger, self-will, and every other evil temper—in a word, changing the 'earthly, sensual, devilish' mind, into 'the mind which was in Christ Jesus'.

Sermon 43: The Scripture Way of Salvation, § I.4

A Hymn from Charles Wesley

There the rough mountains of the deep
Obey thy strong command;
Thy breath can raise the billows steep,
Or sink them to the sand.

Thy glories blaze all nature round,
And strike the wond'ring sight,
Through skies, and seas, and solid ground,
With terror and delight.

Infinite strength and equal skill
Shine through thy works abroad;
Our souls with vast amazement fill,
And speak the builder God!

But the mild glories of thy grace
Our softer passions move;
Pity divine in Jesu's face
We see, adore, and love!

(*Collection*-1781, #217:9-12; CM)

Prayers, Comments & Questions

O God, from your providing hand even the dissatisfied and grumbling receive what they need for their lives. Teach us your ways of justice and lead us to practice your generosity, so that we may live a life worthy of the gospel made known through your Son Jesus Christ, our Savior. Amen.

Sunday between September 25 and October 1 inclusive

27

Preparation for Sunday
Daily: Psalm 78:1-4, 12-16

24 **Thursday**
Isaiah 48:17-21
James 4:11-16

25 **Friday**
Numbers 20:1-13
Acts 13:32-41

26 **Saturday**
Numbers 27:12-14
Mark 11:27-33

Sunday
Exodus 17:1-7
Psalm 78:1-4, 12-16
Philippians 2:1-13
Matthew 21:23-32

Reflection on Sunday
Daily: Psalm 42

28 **Monday**
Exodus 18:1-12
Philippians 1:3-14

29 **Tuesday**
Exodus 18:13-27
Philippians 1:15-21

Wednesday
30 Exodus 19:9b-25
Matthew 9:2-8

The General Rule of Discipleship
*To witness to Jesus Christ in the world and to follow his teachings
through acts of compassion, justice, worship, and devotion under the guidance of the Holy Spirit.*

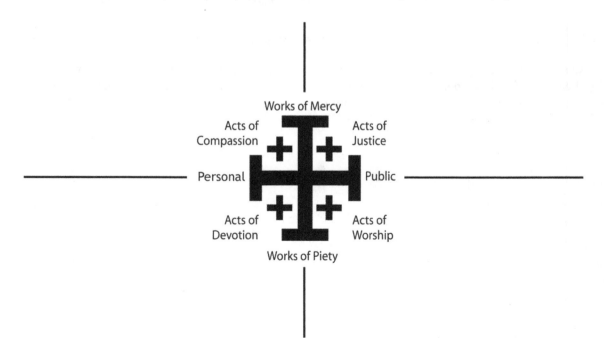

A Word from John Wesley

From the time of our being 'born again' the gradual work of sanctification takes place. We are enabled 'by the Spirit' to 'mortify the deeds of the body', of our evil nature. And as we are more and more dead to sin, we are more and more alive to God. We go on from grace to grace, while we are careful to 'abstain from all appearance of evil', and are 'zealous of good works', 'as we have opportunity doing good to all men'; while we walk in all His ordinances blameless, therein worshiping Him in spirit and in truth; while we take up our cross and deny ourselves every pleasure that does not lead us to God.

Sermon 43: The Scripture Way of Salvation, § I.8

A Hymn from Charles Wesley

Summoned my labour to renew,
And glad to act my part,
Lord, in thy name my work I do,
And with a single heart.

End of my every action thou,
In all things thee I see;
Accept my hallowed labour now;
I do it unto thee.

Whate'er the Father views as thine
He views with gracious eyes;
Jesu, this mean oblation join
To thy great sacrifice.

(*Collection*-1781, #312: 1-3; CM)

Prayers, Comments & Questions

Welcoming God, you receive and bless all who come to you in humility. Show us our false pride, that we may repent of all conceit and arrogance and, caring for one another, may honor Jesus to the glory of your name. Amen.

Oct

Sunday between October 2 and 8 inclusive

Preparation for Sunday
Daily: Psalm 19

Thursday
Exodus 23:1-9
Colossians 2:16-23

Friday
Exodus 23:14-19
Philippians 2:14-18; 3:1-4a

Saturday
Exodus 23:10-13
John 7:40-52

Sunday
Exodus 20:1-4, 7-9, 12-20
Psalm 19
Philippians 3:4b-14
Matthew 21:33-46

Reflection on Sunday
Daily: Psalm 119:49-56

Monday
Deuteronomy 5:1-21
1 Peter 2:4-10

Tuesday
Deuteronomy 5:22—6:3
2 Corinthians 5:17-21

Wednesday
Deuteronomy 6:10-25
John 11:45-57

The General Rule of Discipleship
To witness to Jesus Christ in the world and to follow his teachings
through acts of compassion, justice, worship, and devotion under the guidance of the Holy Spirit.

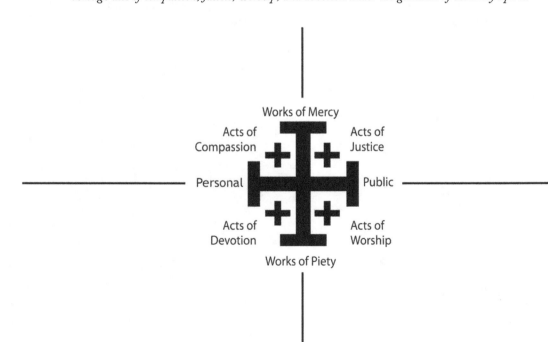

148

A Word from John Wesley

. . . we wait for entire sanctification, for a full salvation from all our sins, from pride, self-will, anger, unbelief; or, as the Apostle expresses it, 'Go on unto perfection.' But what is perfection? The word has various senses: here it means perfect love. It is love excluding sin; love filling the heart, taking up the whole capacity of the soul. It is love 'rejoicing evermore, praying without ceasing, in every thing giving thanks'.

Sermon 43: The Scripture Way of Salvation, § I.9

A Hymn from Charles Wesley

God of almighty love,
By whose sufficient grace
I lift my heart to things above,
And humbly seek thy face;
Through Jesus Christ the just
My faint desires receive,
And let me in thy goodness trust,
And to thy glory live.

Spirit of faith, inspire
My consecrated heart;
Fill me with pure, celestial fire,
With all thou hast and art;
My feeble mind transform,
And, perfectly renewed,
Into a saint exalt a worm—
A worm exalt to God!

(*Collection*-1781, #314: 1& 3; SMD)

Prayers, Comments & Questions

God, our beloved, you set before us the goal of new life in Christ. May we live in the power of his resurrection and bring forth the fruit of your gentle and loving rule. Amen.

Sunday between October 9 and 15 inclusive

Preparation for Sunday
Daily: Psalm 106:1-6, 19-23

Thursday
Exodus 24:1-8
1 Peter 5:1-5, 12-14

Friday
Exodus 24:9-11
James 4:4-10

Saturday
Exodus 24:12-18
Mark 2:18-22

Sunday
Exodus 32:1-14
Psalm 106:1-6, 19-23
Philippians 4:1-9
Matthew 22:1-14

Reflection on Sunday
Daily: Psalm 97

Monday
Exodus 32:15-35
Jude 17-25

Tuesday
Exodus 33:1-6
Philippians 3:13—4:1

Wednesday
2 Kings 17:7-20
John 6:25-35

The General Rule of Discipleship
To witness to Jesus Christ in the world and to follow his teachings
through acts of compassion, justice, worship, and devotion under the guidance of the Holy Spirit.

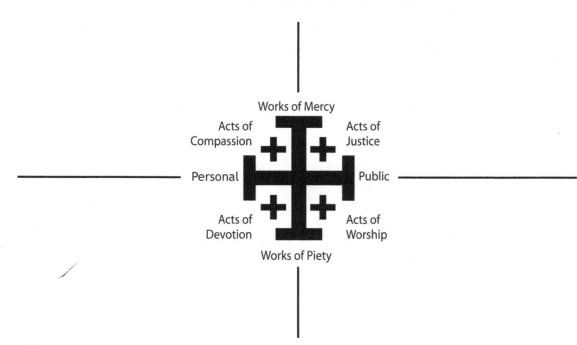

150

A Word from John Wesley

Faith, in general, is defined by the Apostle, - An evidence, A divine evidence and conviction (the word means both) of things not seen; not visible, not perceivable either by sight, or by any other of the external senses. It implies both a supernatural evidence of God, and of the things of God; a kind of spiritual light exhibited to the soul, and a supernatural sight or perception thereof.

Sermon 43: The Scripture Way of Salvation, § II.1

A Hymn from Charles Wesley

O thou who camest from above
The pure celestial fire t'impart,
Kindle a flame of sacred love
On the mean altar of my heart!

There let it for thy glory burn
With inextinguishable blaze,
And trembling to its source return
In humble love, and fervent praise.

Jesu, confirm my heart's desire
To work, and speak, and think for thee;
Still let me guard the holy fire,
And still stir up thy gift in me;

Ready for all thy perfect will,
My acts of faith and love repeat,
Till death thy endless mercies seal,
And make the sacrifice complete.

(*Collection*-1781, #318; LM)

Prayers, Comments & Questions

God of Aaron, Miriam, and Moses, you stayed the hand of your wrath when we fell into idolatry and discord; and when we forgot our deliverance, your love for us remained unchanging. Transform us and our world into a place of justice, love, and peace. Welcome us to your wedding feast where all are invited to be gathered in. Amen.

Sunday between October 16 and 22 inclusive

Preparation for Sunday
Daily: Psalm 99

Thursday
Exodus 33:7-11
3 John 9-12

Friday
Exodus 31:1-11
1 Peter 5:1-5

Saturday
Exodus 39:32-43
Matthew 14:1-12

Sunday
Exodus 33:12-23
Psalm 99
1 Thessalonians 1:1-10
Matthew 22:15-22

Reflection on Sunday
Daily: Psalm 63:1-8

Monday
Exodus 40:34-38
Revelation 18:1-10, 19-20

Tuesday
Numbers 12:1-9
Revelation 18:21-24

Wednesday
Numbers 13:1-2, 17—14:9
Matthew 17:22-27

The General Rule of Discipleship
To witness to Jesus Christ in the world and to follow his teachings through acts of compassion, justice, worship, and devotion under the guidance of the Holy Spirit.

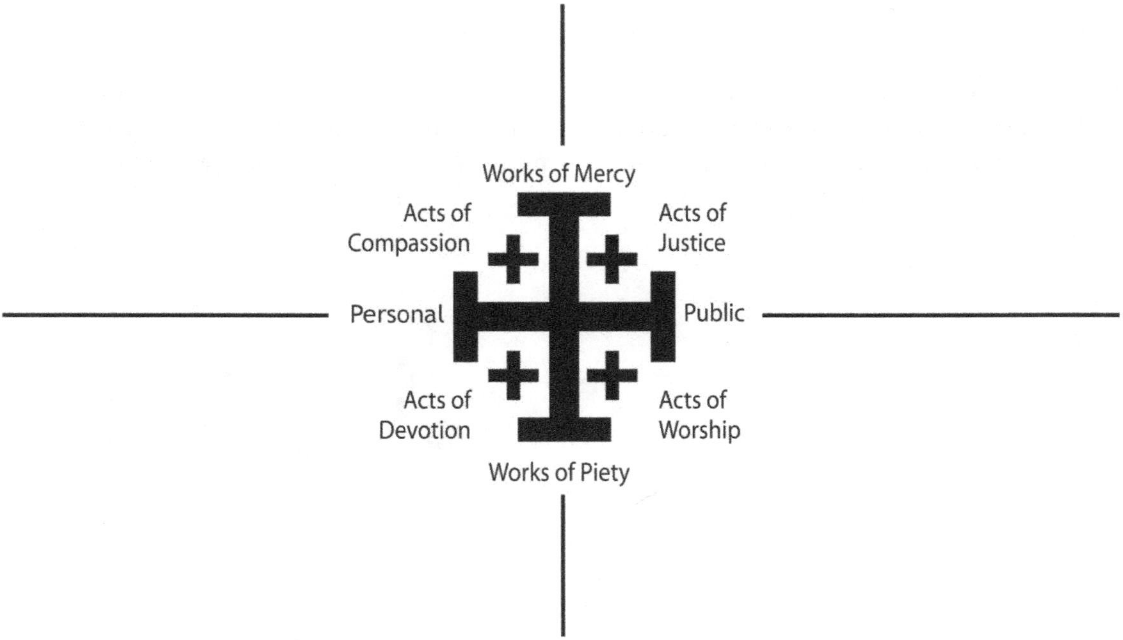

A Word from John Wesley

[Faith is. . .] "God, who commanded light to shine out of darkness, hath shined in our hearts, to give us the light of the knowledge of the glory of God in the face of Jesus Christ." And else where the same Apostle speaks of "the eyes of" our "understanding being opened." By this two-fold operation of the Holy Spirit, having the eyes of our soul both opened and enlightened we see the things which the natural "eye hath not seen, neither the ear heard." We have a prospect of the invisible things of God; we see the spiritual world, which is all round about us, and yet no more discerned by our natural faculties than if it had no being: And we see the eternal world; piercing through the veil which hangs between time and eternity. Clouds and darkness then rest upon it no more, but we already see the glory which shall be revealed.

Sermon 43: The Scripture Way of Salvation, § II.1

A Hymn from Charles Wesley

Forth in thy name, O Lord, I go,
My daily labour to pursue,
Thee, only thee, resolved to know
In all I think, or speak, or do.

The task thy wisdom has assigned
O let me cheerfully fulfill,
In all my works thy presence find,
And prove thy acceptable will.

Thee may I set at my right hand
Whose eyes my inmost substance see,
And labour on at thy command,
And offer all my works to thee.

Give me to bear thy easy yoke,
And every moment watch and pray,
And still to things eternal look,
And hasten to thy glorious day.

For thee delightfully employ
Whate'er thy bounteous grace hath given,
And run my course with even joy,
And closely walk with thee to heaven.

(*Collection*-1781, #315: 1-5; LM)

Prayers, Comments & Questions

You know each of us by name, O God, and in your sight we have found favor, yet our minds cannot comprehend the vision of your glory or the vastness of your love. Grant that as we glimpse your greatness, reflected in your many gifts, we may always return to you the praise that is yours alone. We ask this through Jesus Christ our Lord. Amen.

Sunday between October 23 and 29 inclusive

Preparation for Sunday
Daily: Psalm 90:1-6, 13-17

Thursday
Deuteronomy 31:14-22
Titus 1:5-16

Friday
Deuteronomy 32:1-14, 18
Titus 2:7-8, 11-15

Saturday
Deuteronomy 32:44-47
John 5:39-47

Sunday
Deuteronomy 34:1-12
Psalm 90:1-6, 13-17
1 Thessalonians 2:1-8
Matthew 22:34-46

Reflection on Sunday
Daily: Psalm 119:41-48

Monday
Numbers 33:38-39
James 2:8-13

Tuesday
Exodus 34:29-35
James 2:14-26

Wednesday
Deuteronomy 26:16—27:7
Matthew 19:16-22

The General Rule of Discipleship
To witness to Jesus Christ in the world and to follow his teachings
through acts of compassion, justice, worship, and devotion under the guidance of the Holy Spirit.

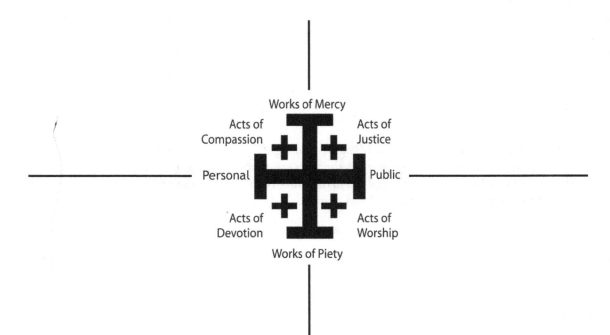

A Word from John Wesley

. . . faith is a divine evidence and conviction, not only that "God was in Christ, reconciling the world unto himself," but also that Christ loved me, and gave himself for me. It is by this faith (whether we term it the essence, or rather a property thereof) that we receive Christ; that we receive him in all his offices, as our Prophet, Priest, and King. It is by this that he is "made of God unto us wisdom, and righteousness, and sanctification, and redemption."

Sermon 43: The Scripture Way of Salvation, § II.2

A Hymn from Charles Wesley

Try us, O God, and search the ground
Of every sinful heart!
Whate'er of sin in us is found,
O bid it all depart!

When to the right or left we stray,
Leave us not comfortless,
But guide our feet into the way
Of everlasting peace.

Help us to help each other, Lord,
Each other's cross to bear;
Let each his friendly aid afford,
And feel his brother's care.

Help us to build each other up,
Our little stock improve;
Increase our faith, confirm our hope,
And perfect us in love.

(*Collection*-1781, #489: 1-4; CM)

Prayers, Comments & Questions

Almighty God, your Son has shown us how to love one another. May our love for you overflow into joyous service and be a healing witness to our neighbors through Jesus Christ our Lord. Amen.

Sunday between October 30 and November 5 inclusive

Handwritten: 12 Priest - each 1 tribe - carried ark across
Now carrying the ark across Jordan - dried up - → Jericho

Preparation for Sunday
Daily: Psalm 107:1-7, 33-37

Thursday *"lead people to promised land"*
29
✓ Joshua 1:1-11
Romans 2:17-29

Friday
30
✓ Joshua 2:1-14
2 Peter 2:1-3

Saturday *spied out the country - 2 women hid the spies for safety*
31
Joshua 2:15-24
Matthew 23:13-28

Sunday
Joshua 3:7-17
Psalm 107:1-7, 33-37
1 Thessalonians 2:9-13
Matthew 23:1-12

Reflection on Sunday
Daily: Psalm 128

12 stones from Jordan were placed where the ark stood
Monday
2
Joshua 4:1-24
1 Thessalonians 2:13-20

Then circling walls of Jericho 7 times - the walls fall! from trumpet blowing + shouting
Tuesday
3
Joshua 6:1-16, 20
Acts 13:1-12

Wednesday
4
Joshua 10:12-14
Matthew 15:1-9

The General Rule of Discipleship
*To witness to Jesus Christ in the world and to follow his teachings
through acts of compassion, justice, worship, and devotion under the guidance of the Holy Spirit.*

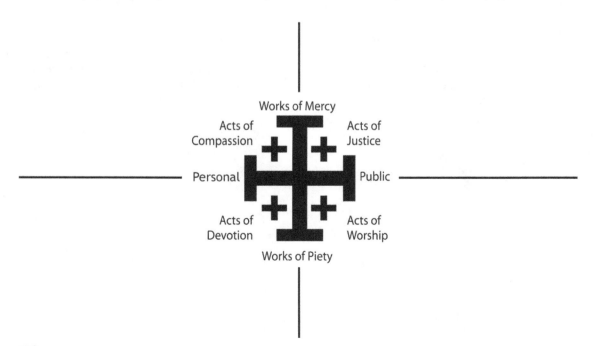

Works of Mercy

Acts of Compassion — Acts of Justice

Personal — Public

Acts of Devotion — Acts of Worship

Works of Piety

A Word from John Wesley

The Apostle says, "There is one faith, and one hope of our calling;" one Christian, saving faith; "as there is one Lord," in whom we believe, and "one God and Father of us all." And it is certain, this faith necessarily implies an assurance (which is here only another word for evidence, it being hard to tell the difference between them) that Christ loved me, and gave himself for me.

Sermon 43: The Scripture Way of Salvation, § II.3

A Hymn from Charles Wesley

Jesu, united by thy grace,
And each to each endeared,
With confidence we seek thy face,
And know our prayer is heard.

Still let us own our common Lord,
And bear thine easy yoke,
A band of love, a threefold cord
Which never can be broke.

Make us into one Spirit drink,
Baptize into thy name,
And let us always kindly think,
And sweetly speak the same.

Touched by the loadstone of thy love,
Let all our hearts agree,
And ever towards each other move,
And ever move towards thee.

(*Collection*-1781, #490: 1-4; CM)

Prayers, Comments & Questions

Your steadfast love endures from age to age, O living God, for in Christ you tenderly care for your people. Instruct us in your way of humble service, that we may imitate his saving deeds who humbled himself for our salvation and is now exalted with you in splendor for ever and ever. Amen.

Sunday between November 6 and 12 inclusive

Preparation for Sunday
Daily: Psalm 78:1-7

Thursday
Joshua 5:10-12
Revelation 8:6—9:12

Friday
Joshua 8:30-35
Revelation 9:13-21

Saturday
Joshua 20:1-9
Matthew 24:1-14

Sunday
Joshua 24:1-3a, 14-25
Psalm 78:1-7
1 Thessalonians 4:13-18
Matthew 25:1-13

Reflection on Sunday
Daily: Psalm 78

Monday
Joshua 24:25-33
1 Corinthians 14:20-25

Tuesday
Nehemiah 8:1-12
1 Thessalonians 3:6-13

Wednesday
Jeremiah 31:31-34
Matthew 24:29-35

The General Rule of Discipleship
To witness to Jesus Christ in the world and to follow his teachings
through acts of compassion, justice, worship, and devotion under the guidance of the Holy Spirit.

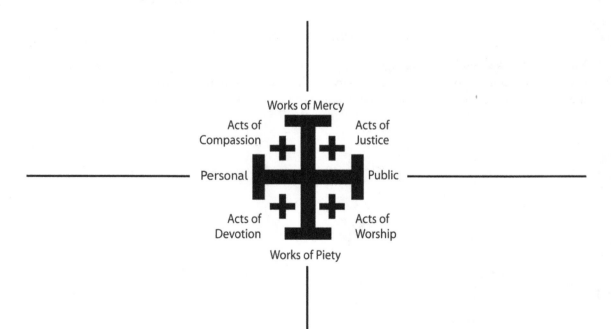

A Word from John Wesley

For "he that believeth" with the true living faith, "hath the witness in himself:" "The Spirit witnesseth with his spirit, that he is a child of God." "Because he is a son, God hath sent forth the Spirit of his Son into his heart, crying, Abba, Father;" giving him an assurance that he is so, and a childlike confidence in him. But let it be observed, that, in the very nature of the thing, the assurance goes before the confidence. For a man cannot have a childlike confidence in God till he knows he is a child of God. Therefore confidence, trust, reliance, adherence, or whatever else it be called, is not the first, as some have supposed, but the second branch or act of faith.

Sermon 43: The Scripture Way of Salvation, § II.3

A Hymn from Charles Wesley

To thee inseparably joined,
Let all our spirits cleave;
O may we all the loving mind
That was in thee receive!

This is the bond of perfectness,
Thy spotless charity;
O let us (still we pray) possess
The mind that was in thee!

Grant this, and then from all below
Insensibly remove;
Our souls their change shall scarcely know,
Made perfect first in love!

With ease our souls through death shall glide
Into their paradise,
And thence on wings of angels ride
Triumphant through the skies.

Yet when the fullest joy is given,
The same delight we prove,
In earth, in paradise, in heaven
Our all in all is love.

(*Collection*-1781, #490:5-9; CM)

Prayers, Comments & Questions

You let us choose, O God, between you and the false gods of this world. In the midst of the night of sin and death, wake us from our slumber and call us forth to greet Christ so that with eyes and hearts fixed on him, we may follow to eternal light. Amen.

Sunday between November 13 and 19 inclusive

Preparation for Sunday
Daily: Psalm 123

Thursday
Judges 2:6-15
Revelation 16:1-7

Friday
Judges 2:16-23
Revelation 16:8-21

Saturday
Judges 5:1-12
Matthew 12:43-45

Sunday
Judges 4:1-7
Psalm 123
1 Thessalonians 5:1-11
Matthew 25:14-30

Reflection on Sunday
Daily: Psalm 83:1-4, 9-10, 17-18

Monday
Judges 4:8-24
Romans 2:1-11

Tuesday
Exodus 2:1-10
1 Thessalonians 5:12-18

Wednesday
Esther 7:1-10
Matthew 24:45-51

The General Rule of Discipleship
To witness to Jesus Christ in the world and to follow his teachings
through acts of compassion, justice, worship, and devotion under the guidance of the Holy Spirit.

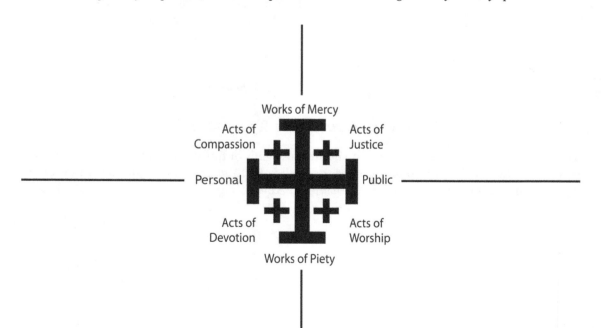

Works of Mercy

Acts of Compassion — Acts of Justice

Personal — Public

Acts of Devotion — Acts of Worship

Works of Piety

A Word from John Wesley

How are we justified by faith? In what sense is this to be understood? I answer, Faith is the condition, and the only condition, of justification. It is the condition: None is justified but he that believes: Without faith no man is justified. And it is the only condition: This alone is sufficient for justification. Every one that believes is justified, whatever else he has or has not. In other words: No man is justified till he believes; every man, when he believes, is justified.

Sermon 43: The Scripture Way of Salvation, § III.1

A Hymn from Charles Wesley

What shall we offer our good Lord,
Poor nothings! for his boundless grace?
Fain would we his great name record,
And worthily set forth his praise.

Great object of our growing love,
To whom our more than all we owe,
Open the fountain from above,
And let it our full souls o'erflow.

So shall our lives thy power proclaim,
Thy grace for every sinner free;
Till all mankind shall learn thy name,
Shall all stretch out their hands to thee!

Open a door which earth and hell
May strive to shut, but strive in vain;
Let thy word richly in us dwell,
And let our gracious fruit remain!

(*Collection*-1781, #479:1-4; LM)

Prayers, Comments & Questions

God of the covenant, even when we fall into sin, your Spirit invites us to remember that you chose us to be your servant people. Awaken us to the power of gifts you pour into us for the good of creation, and grant that we may be trustworthy in all things, producing abundantly as we work to build your realm. Amen.

Sunday between November 20 and 26 inclusive
Christ the King

Preparation for Sunday
Daily: Psalm 100

Thursday
Genesis 48:15-22
Revelation 14:1-11

Friday
Isaiah 40:1-11
Revelation 22:1-9

Saturday
Ezekiel 34:25-31
Matthew 12:46-50

Sunday
Ezekiel 34:11-16, 20-24
Psalm 100
Ephesians 1:15-23
Matthew 25:31-46

Reflection on Sunday
Daily: Psalm 28

Monday
Numbers 27:15-23
2 Timothy 2:8-13

Tuesday
Zechariah 11:4-17
Revelation 19:1-9

Wednesday
Jeremiah 31:10-14
John 5:19-40

The General Rule of Discipleship
To witness to Jesus Christ in the world and to follow his teachings
through acts of compassion, justice, worship, and devotion under the guidance of the Holy Spirit.

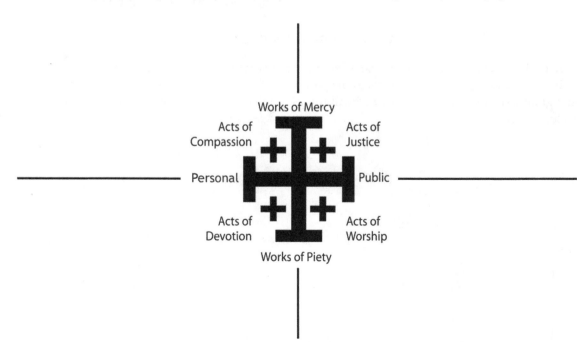

A Word from John Wesley

God does undoubtedly command us both to repent, and to bring forth fruits meet for repentance; which if we willingly neglect, we cannot reasonably expect to be justified at all: Therefore both repentance, and fruits meet for repentance, are, in some sense, necessary to justification. But they are not necessary in the same sense with faith, nor in the same degree. Not in the same degree; for those fruits are only necessary conditionally; if there be time and opportunity for them. Otherwise a man may be justified without them, as was the thief upon the cross; but he cannot be justified without faith; this is impossible.

Sermon 43: The Scripture Way of Salvation, § III.2

A Hymn from Charles Wesley

Partners of a glorious hope,
Lift your hearts and voices up.
Jointly let us rise and sing
Christ our Prophet, Priest, and King.
Monuments of Jesu's grace,
Speak we by our lives his praise,
Walk in him we have received,
Show we not in vain believed.

Hence may all our actions flow,
Love the proof that Christ we know;
Mutual love the token be,
Lord, that we belong to thee.
Love, thine image love impart!
Stamp it on our face and heart!
Only love to us be given—
Lord, we ask no other heaven.

(*Collection*-1781, #508:1, 4; 77.77 D)

Prayers, Comments & Questions

You raised up your Son, O God, and seated him at your right hand as the shepherd and king who seeks what is lost, binds up what is wounded, and strengthens what is weak. Empowered by the Spirit, grant that we may share with others that which we have received from your hand, to the honor of Jesus Christ. Amen.

Articles

Advice to the People Called Methodists

John Wesley

It may be needful to specify whom I mean by this ambiguous term; since it would be lost labour to speak to Methodists, so called, without first describing those to whom I speak. By Methodists I mean, a people who profess to pursue (in whatsoever measure they have attained) holiness of heart and life, inward and outward conformity in all things to the revealed will of God; who place religion in an uniform resemblance of the great object of it; in a steady imitation of Him they worship, in all his imitable perfections; more particularly, in justice, mercy, and truth, or universal love filling the heart, and governing the life.

You, to whom I now speak, believe this love of human kind cannot spring but from the love of God. You think there can be no instance of one whose tender affection embraces every child of man, (though not endeared to him either by ties of blood, or by any natural or civil relation,) unless that affection flow from a grateful, filial love to the common Father of all; to God, considered not only as his Father, but as "the Father of the spirits of all flesh;" yea, as the general Parent and Friend of all the families both of heaven and earth.

This filial love you suppose to flow only from faith, which you describe as a supernatural evidence (or conviction) of things not seen; so that to him who has this principle,

> The things unknown to feeble sense,
> Unseen by reason's glimmering ray,
> With strong commanding evidence
> Their heavenly origin display.
> Faith lends its realizing light,
> The clouds disperse, the shadows fly;
> The' Invisible appears in sight,
> And God is seen by mortal eye.

You suppose this faith to imply an evidence that God is merciful to me a sinner; that he is reconciled to me by the death of his Son, and now accepts me for his sake. You accordingly describe the faith of a real Christian as "a sure trust and confidence" (over and above his assent to the sacred writings) "which he hath in God, that his sins are forgiven; and that he is, through the merits of Christ, reconciled to the favour of God."

You believe, farther, that both this faith and love are wrought in us by the Spirit of God; nay, that there cannot be in any man one good temper or desire, or so much as one good thought, unless it be produced by the almighty power of God, by the inspiration or influence of the Holy Ghost. If you walk by this rule, continually endeavouring to know and love and resemble and obey the great God and Father of our Lord Jesus Christ, as the God of love, of pardoning mercy; if from this principle of loving, obedient faith, you carefully abstain from all evil, and labour, as you have opportunity, to do good to all men, friends or enemies; if, lastly, you unite together, to encourage and help each other in thus working out your salvation, and for that end watch over one another in love, you are they whom I mean by Methodists.

The First general advice which one who loves your souls would earnestly recommend to every one of you is: "Consider, with deep and frequent attention, the peculiar circumstances wherein you stand."

One of these is, that you are a new people: Your name is new, (at least, as used in a religious sense,) not heard of, till a few years ago, either in our own or any other nation. Your principles are new, in this respect, that there is no other set of people among us (and, possibly, not in the Christian world) who hold them all in the same degree and connexion; who so strenuously and continually insist on the absolute necessity of universal holiness both in heart and life; of a peaceful, joyous love of God; of a supernatural evidence of things not seen; of an inward witness that we are the children of God; and of the inspiration of the Holy Ghost, in order to any good thought, or word, or work. And perhaps there is no other set of people, (at least, not visibly united together,) who lay so much and yet no more stress than you do on rectitude of opinions, on outward modes of worship, and the use of those ordinances which you acknowledge to be of God. So much stress you lay even on right opinions, as to profess, that you earnestly desire to have a right judgment in all things, and are glad to use every means which you know or believe may be conducive thereto; and yet not so much as to condemn any man upon earth, merely for thinking otherwise than you do; much less, to imagine that God condemns him for this, if he be upright and sincere of heart. On those outward modes of worship, wherein you have been bred up, you lay so much stress as highly to approve them; but not so much as to lessen your love to those who conscientiously dissent from you herein. You likewise lay so much stress on the use of those ordinances which you believe to be of God, as to confess there is no salvation for you if you wilfully neglect them: And yet you do not judge them that are otherwise minded; you determine nothing concerning those who, not believing those ordinances to be of God, do, out of principle, abstain from them.

Your strictness of life, taking the whole of it together, may likewise be accounted new. I mean, your making it a rule, to abstain from fashionable diversions, from reading plays, romances, or books of humour, from singing innocent songs, or talking in a merry, gay, diverting manner; your plainness of dress; your manner of dealing in trade; your exactness in observing the Lord's day; your scrupulosity as to things that have not paid custom; your total abstinence from spirituous liquors (unless in cases of necessity); your rule, "not to mention the fault of an absent person, in particular of Ministers or of those in authority," may justly be termed new: Seeing, although some are scrupulous in some of these things, and others are strict with regard to other particulars, yet we do not find any other body of people who insist on all these rules together. With respect, therefore, both to your name, principles, and practice, you may be considered as a new people.

Another peculiar circumstance of your present situation is, that you are newly united together; that you are just gathered, or (as it seems) gathering rather, out of all other societies or congregations; nay, and that you have been hitherto, and do still subsist, without power, (for you are a low, insignificant people,) without riches, (for you are poor almost to a man, having no more than the plain necessaries of life,) and without either any extraordinary gifts of nature, or the advantages of education; most even of your Teachers being quite unlearned, and (in other things) ignorant men.

There is yet another circumstance, which is quite peculiar to yourselves: Whereas every other religious set of people, as soon as they were joined to each other, separated themselves from their former societies or congregations; you, on the contrary, do not; nay, you absolutely disavow all desire of separating from them. You openly and continually declare you have not, nor ever had, such a design. And whereas the congregations to which those separatists belonged have generally spared no pains to prevent that separation; those to which you belong spare no pains (not to prevent, but) to occasion this separation, to drive you from them, to force you on that division to which you declare you have the strongest aversion. Considering these peculiar circumstances wherein you stand, you will see the propriety of a Second advice I would recommend to you: "Do not imagine you can avoid giving offence:" Your very name renders this impossible. Perhaps not one in a hundred of those who use the term Methodist have any ideas of what it means. To ninety-nine of them it is still heathen Greek. Only they think it means something very bad, either a Papist, a heretic, an underminer of the Church, or some unheard-of monster; and, in all probability, the farther it goes, it must gather up more and more evil. It is vain, therefore, for any that is called a Methodist ever to think of not giving offence.

And as much offence as you give by your name, you will give still more by your principles. You will give offence to the bigots for opinions, modes of worship, and ordinances, by laying no more stress upon them; to the bigots against them, by laying so much; to men of form, by insisting so frequently and strongly on the inward power of religion; to moral men, (so called,) by declaring the absolute necessity of faith, in order to acceptance with God. To men of reason you will give offence, by talking of inspiration and receiving the Holy Ghost; to drunkards, Sabbath-breakers, common swearers, and other open sinners, by refraining from their company, as well as by that disapprobation of their behaviour which you will often be obliged to express. And indeed your life must give them continual offence: Your sobriety is grievously offensive to a drunkard; your serious conversation is equally intolerable to a gay impertinent: and, in general, that "you are grown so precise and singular, so monstrously strict, beyond all sense and reason, that you scruple so many harmless things, and fancy you are obliged to do so many others which you need not," cannot but be an offence to abundance of people, your friends and relations in particular. Either, therefore, you must consent to give up your principles, or your fond hope of pleasing men.

What makes even your principles more offensive is, this uniting of yourselves together: Because this union renders you more conspicuous, placing you more in the eye of men; more suspicious, I mean, liable to be suspected of carrying on some sinister design (especially by those who do not, or will not, know your inviolable attachment to His present Majesty); more dreadful, to those of a fearful temper, who imagine you have any such design; and more odious to men of zeal, if their zeal be any other than fervent love to God and man.

This offence will sink the deeper, because you are gathered out of so many other congregations: For the warm men in each will not easily be convinced, that you do not despise either them or their teachers; nay, will probably imagine, that you utterly condemn them, as though they could not be saved. And this occasion of offence is now at the height, because you are just gathered, or gathering rather, so that they know not where it will end; but the fear of losing (so they account it) more of their members, gives an edge to their zeal, and keeps all their anger and resentment in its strength.

Add to this, that you do not leave them quite, you still rank yourselves among their members; which, to those who know not that you do it for conscience' sake, is also a provoking circumstance. "If you would but get out of their sight!" But you are a continual thorn in their side, as long as you remain with them.

And (which cannot but anger them the more) you have neither power, nor riches, nor learning; yet, with all their power, and money, and wisdom, they can gain no ground against you.

You cannot but expect, that the offence continually arising from such a variety of provocations will gradually ripen into hatred, malice, and all other unkind tempers. And as they who are thus affected will not fail to represent you to others in the same light as you appear to them, sometimes as madmen and fools, sometimes as wicked men, fellows not fit to live upon the earth; the consequence, humanly speaking, must be, that, together with your reputation, you will lose, first, the love of your friends, relations, and acquaintance, even those who once loved you the most tenderly; then your business, for many will employ you no longer, nor "buy of such an one as you are;" and, in due time, (unless He who governs the world interpose,) your health, liberty, and life.

What further advice can be given to persons in such a situation? I cannot but advise you, Thirdly, "Consider deeply with yourself, Is the God whom I serve able to deliver me? I am not able to deliver myself out of these difficulties; much less am I able to bear them. I know not how to give up my reputation, my friends, my substance, my liberty, my life. Can God give me to rejoice in doing this; and may I depend upon him that he will? Are the hairs of my head all numbered; and does He never fail them that trust in him?" Weigh this thoroughly; and if you can trust God with your all, then go on in the power of his might.

Go on, I would earnestly advise you, Fourthly: "Keep in the very path wherein you now tread. Be true to your principles." Never rest again in the dead formality of religion. Pursue with your might inward and outward holiness; a steady imitation of Him you worship; a still increasing resemblance of his imitable perfections, his justice, mercy, and truth.

Let this be your manly, noble, generous religion, equally remote from the meanness of superstition, which places religion in doing what God hath not enjoined, or abstaining from what he hath not forbidden; and from the unkindness of bigotry, which confines our affection to our own party, sect, or opinion. Above all, stand fast in obedient faith, faith in the God of pardoning mercy, in the God and Father of our Lord Jesus Christ, who hath loved you, and given himself for you. Ascribe to Him all the good you find in yourself; all your peace, and joy, and love; all your power to do and suffer his will, through the Spirit of the living God. Yet, in the mean time, carefully avoid enthusiasm: Impute not the dreams of men to the all-wise God; and expect neither light nor power from him, but in the serious use of all the means he hath ordained.

Be true also to your principles touching opinions and the externals of religion. Use every ordinance which you believe is of God; but beware of narrowness of spirit towards those who use them not. Conform yourself to those modes of worship which you approve; yet love as brethren those who cannot conform. Lay so much stress on opinions, that all your own, if it be possible, may agree with truth and reason; but have a care of anger, dislike, or contempt towards those whose opinions differ from yours. You are daily accused of this; (and, indeed, what is it whereof you are not accused?) but beware of giving any ground for such an accusation. Condemn no man for not thinking as you think: Let every one enjoy the full and free liberty of thinking for himself: Let every man use his own judgment, since every man must give an account of himself to God. Abhor every approach, in any kind or degree, to the spirit of persecution. If you cannot reason or persuade a man into the truth, never attempt to force him into it. If love will not compel him to come in, leave him to God, the Judge of all. Yet expect not that others will deal thus with you. No: Some will endeavour to fright you out of your principles; some to shame you into a more popular religion, to laugh and rally you out of your singularity: But from none of these will you be in so great danger, as from those who assault you with quite different weapons; with softness, good-nature, and earnest professions of (perhaps real) good-will. Here you are equally concerned to avoid the very appearance of anger, contempt, or unkindness, and to hold fast the whole truth of God, both in principle and in practice.

This indeed will be interpreted as unkindness. Your former acquaintance will look upon this, that you will not sin or trifle with them, as a plain proof of your coldness towards them; and this burden you must be content to bear: But labour to avoid all real unkindness, all disobliging words, or harshness of speech, all shyness, or strangeness of behaviour. Speak to them with all the tenderness and love, and behave with all the sweetness and courtesy, you can; taking care not to give any needless offence to neighbour or stranger, friend or enemy.

Perhaps on this very account I might advise you, Fifthly, "not to talk much of what you suffer; of the persecution you endured at such a time, and the wickedness of your persecutors." Nothing more tends to exasperate them than this; and therefore (although there is a time when these things must be mentioned, yet) it might be a general rule, to do it as seldom as you can with a safe conscience. For, besides its tendency to inflame them, it has the appearance of evil, of ostentation, of magnifying yourselves. It also tends to puff you up with pride, and to make you think yourselves some great ones, as it certainly does to excite or increase in your heart ill-will, anger, and all unkind tempers. It is, at best, loss of time; for, instead of the wickedness of men, you might be talking of the goodness of God. Nay, it is, in truth, an open, wilful sin: It is tale-bearing, back-biting, evil-speaking, a sin you can never be sufficiently watchful against, seeing it steals upon you in a thousand shapes. Would it not be far more profitable for your souls, instead of speaking against them, to pray for them? to confirm your love towards those unhappy men, whom you believe to be fighting against God, by crying mightily to him in their behalf, that he may open their eyes and change their hearts?

I have now only to commend you to the care of Him who hath all power in heaven and in earth; beseeching Him, that, in every circumstance of life, you may stand "firm as the beaten anvil to the stroke;" desiring nothing on earth; accounting all things but dung and dross, that you may win Christ; and always remembering, "It is the part of a good champion, to be flayed alive, and to conquer!"

October 10, 1745

The Nature, Design, and General Rules of Our United Societies

In the latter end of the year 1739 eight or ten persons came to Mr. Wesley, in London, who appeared to be deeply convinced of sin, and earnestly groaning for redemption. They desired, as did two or three more the next day, that he would spend some time with them in prayer, and advise them how to flee from the wrath to come, which they saw continually hanging over their heads. That he might have more time for this great work, he appointed a day when they might all come together, which from thenceforward they did every week, namely, on Thursday in the evening. To these, and as many more as desired to join with them (for their number increased daily), he gave those advices from time to time which he judged most needful for them, and they always concluded their meeting with prayer suited to their several necessities.

This was the rise of the **United Society**, first in Europe, and then in America. Such a society is no other than "a company of men having the *form* and seeking the *power* of godliness, united in order to pray together, to receive the word of exhortation, and to watch over one another in love, that they may help each other to work out their salvation."

That it may the more easily be discerned whether they are indeed working out their own salvation, each society is divided into smaller companies, called **classes**, according to their respective places of abode. There are about twelve persons in a class, one of whom is styled the **leader**. It is his duty:

1. To see each person in his class once a week at least, in order:
   - to inquire how their souls prosper;
   - to advise, reprove, comfort or exhort, as occasion may require;
   - to receive what they are willing to give toward the relief of the preachers, church, and poor.

2. To meet the ministers and the stewards of the society once a week, in order:
   - to inform the minister of any that are sick, or of any that walk disorderly and will not be reproved;
   - to pay the stewards what they have received of their several classes in the week preceding.

There is only one condition previously required of those who desire admission into these societies: "a desire to flee from the wrath to come, and to be saved from their sins." But wherever this is really fixed in the soul it will be shown by its fruits.

It is therefore expected of all who continue therein that they should continue to evidence their desire of salvation,

First: By doing no harm, by avoiding evil of every kind, especially that which is most generally practiced, such as:

- The taking of the name of God in vain.
- The profaning the day of the Lord, either by doing ordinary work therein or by buying or selling.
- Drunkenness: buying or selling spirituous liquors, or drinking them, unless in cases of extreme necessity.
- Slaveholding; buying or selling slaves.
- Fighting, quarreling, brawling, brother going to law with brother; returning evil for evil, or railing for railing; the using many words in buying or selling.
- The buying or selling goods that have not paid the duty.
- The giving or taking things on usury—i.e., unlawful interest.
- Uncharitable or unprofitable conversation; particularly speaking evil of magistrates or of ministers.
- Doing to others as we would not they should do unto us.
- Doing what we know is not for the glory of God, as:
  » The putting on of gold and costly apparel.
  » The taking such diversions as cannot be used in the name of the Lord Jesus.
  » The singing those songs, or reading those books, which do not tend to the knowledge or love of God.
  » Softness and needless self-indulgence.
  » Laying up treasure upon earth.
  » Borrowing without a probability of paying; or taking up goods without a probability of paying for them.

It is expected of all who continue in these societies that they should continue to evidence their desire of salvation,

Secondly: By doing good; by being in every kind merciful after their power; as they have opportunity, doing good of every possible sort, and, as far as possible, to all men:

To their bodies, of the ability which God giveth, by giving food to the hungry, by clothing the naked, by visiting or helping them that are sick or in prison.

To their souls, by instructing, reproving, or exhorting all we have any intercourse with; trampling under foot that enthusiastic doctrine that "we are not to do good unless our hearts be free to it."

By doing good, especially to them that are of the household of faith or groaning so to be; employing them preferably to others; buying one of another, helping each other in business, and so much the more because the world will love its own and them only.

By all possible diligence and frugality, that the gospel be not blamed.

By running with patience the race which is set before them, denying themselves, and taking up their cross daily; submitting to bear the reproach of Christ, to be as the filth and offscouring of the world; and looking that men should say all manner of evil of them falsely, for the Lord's sake.

It is expected of all who desire to continue in these societies that they should continue to evidence their desire of salvation,

Thirdly: By attending upon all the ordinances of God; such are:

- The public worship of God.
- The ministry of the Word, either read or expounded.
- The Supper of the Lord.
- Family and private prayer.
- Searching the Scriptures.
- Fasting or abstinence.

These are the General Rules of our societies; all of which we are taught of God to observe, even in his written Word, which is the only rule, and the sufficient rule, both of our faith and practice. And all these we know his Spirit writes on truly awakened hearts. If there be any among us who observe them not, who habitually break any of them, let it be known unto them who watch over that soul as they who must give an account. We will admonish him of the error of his ways. We will bear with him for a season. But then, if he repent not, he hath no more place among us. We have delivered our own souls.

The General Rule of Discipleship

The General Rule of Discipleship is a contemporary re-statement of the General Rules. It distills the General Rules down to a single, straightforward statement that can be easily memorized:

> **To witness to Jesus Christ in the world and to**
> **follow his teachings through acts of**
> **compassion, justice, worship, and devotion**
> **under the guidance of the Holy Spirit.**

The General Rule of Discipleship is a succinct description of discipleship. It begins by acknowledging that a disciple is one who is a witness to Jesus Christ. This tells us that he or she knows Jesus and can tell others who he is and what he is doing in the world.

A disciple lives and witnesses to Jesus Christ in the world. This acknowledges that discipleship is not primarily about the enjoyment of personal blessings. It is much more about joining Christ and his mission in the world. When Christ calls us to follow him, he calls us to follow him into the world he loves.

A disciple follows Jesus by obeying his teachings. The General Rule tells us that discipleship is a relationship with Christ. Disciples participate in practices that draw them to Christ and keep them with him. Jesus said in Luke 9:23,

> "If any want to become my followers, let them deny themselves and take
> up their cross daily and follow me."

Self-denial is loving the way Jesus loves. In the context of discipleship grace enables you to love as God loves.

The cross disciples must take up each day is obedience to Jesus' teachings summarized in Matthew 22:37-40,

> "You shall love the LORD your God with all your heart, and with all your
> soul, and with all your mind." This is the greatest and first command-
> ment. And a second is like it: "You shall love your neighbor as yourself."
> On these two commandments hang all the Law and the Prophets.

Disciples practice loving God (the cross' vertical axis) through acts of worship and devotion. They respond to God's love by loving those whom God loves, as God loves them through acts of compassion and justice (the cross' horizontal axis). As disciples take up the cross of obedience to Jesus' commands they open themselves to grace and grow in holiness of heart and life.

Finally, the General Rule of Discipleship tells us that witnessing to Jesus Christ in the world and following his teachings are guided by the Holy Spirit. This tells us that disciples cannot follow Jesus alone, by their own strength. Only the Holy Spirit, working in them by grace, makes discipleship and subsequent growth in holiness of heart and life possible.

The General Rule of Discipleship helps disciples to maintain balance between all the teachings of Jesus. This balance is represented by the Jerusalem cross (below). The support and accountability provided by a Covenant Discipleship group helps disciples to walk with Christ in the world by practicing both works of mercy (loving the neighbor) and works of piety (loving God). It also helps to maintain balance between the personal and public dimensions of discipleship.

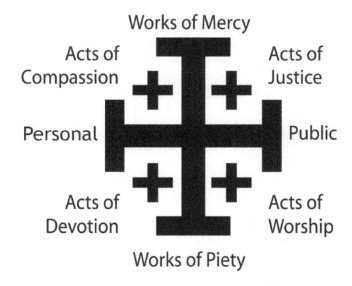

777

Covenant Discipleship Groups

Covenant

. . . is God's word for "relationship." Covenant is God's way of **love**. Covenant tells us that God seeks and keeps relationships with others. The nature of God's covenant is self-giving love. Jesus Christ is God's covenant love in flesh and blood. We experience this love as **grace**; responsible grace. It is God's hand, open and outstretched to the world.

Christians are people who accept God's offer of covenant love in the water of baptism. They respond by turning away from sin and accepting the freedom and power God gives to resist evil. They confess Jesus Christ as Savior, put all their trust in his grace, and promise to serve him as Lord within the community of the church. Christians understand that the life of covenant love cannot be lived alone; it requires a community of prayer, forgiveness, and love.

Christians are covenant people.

Discipleship

. . . is how Christians live out their covenant with God. It is the way of life shaped by the teachings of Jesus Christ, summarized by him in Mark 12:30-31:

> "You shall love the Lord your God with all your heart, and with all your
> soul, and with all your mind, and with all your strength. . . . You shall
> love your neighbor as yourself."

A *disciple* is a person striving to conform his or her life to the life of a beloved teacher. A disciple seeks to become *like* the teacher. Disciples of Jesus Christ are Christians who align their own desires, goals, and habits with the desires, goals, and habits of Jesus Christ.

The apostle Paul describes the goal of discipleship in Philippians 2:5,

> "Let the same mind be in you that was in Christ Jesus."

Groups

. . . are discipleship incubators. It takes a community of love and forgiveness to make disciples.

Jesus gave his disciples a new commandment:

> "Love one another. Just as I have loved you, you also should love one
> another. By this everyone will know that you are my disciples, if you have
> love for one another." (John 13:34-35)

Disciples obey this new commandment when they meet regularly in small groups. They pray for one another, the church and the world. They also give an account of how they have walked with Jesus in the world since they last met. The group works together to help one another become more dependable and mature disciples of Jesus Christ; and leaders in discipleship for the church's mission in the world.

Wesleyan Disciple-Making

Small groups that focus on mutual accountability and support for discipleship are the "method" of Methodism. These groups have their roots firmly planted in the Wesleyan tradition. The roots go even deeper when you consider that John Wesley described Methodism as his attempt to re-tradition "primitive" Christianity. He said

> "a Methodist is one who has 'the love of God shed abroad in his heart
> by the Holy Ghost given unto him (or her)'"—from "The Character of a
> Methodist"

Covenant Discipleship groups are a way of helping Christians to grow in loving God with all their heart, soul, mind, and strength and love their neighbor as themselves. They are a proven and effective way of forming **leaders in discipleship** who in turn disciple others and help the congregation to live out its mission with Christ in the world.

Covenant Discipleship groups form Christ-centered people who lead Christ-centered congregations that participate in Christ's on-going work of preparing the world for the coming reign of God, on earth as it is in heaven (Matthew 6:10; Luke 11:2).

The General Rule of Discipleship

. . . helps Covenant Discipleship group members to practice a balanced and varied discipleship. The General Rule is a contemporary re-statement of The General Rules John Wesley developed for the Methodist societies in 1742. It is simple and elegant:

> **"To witness to Jesus Christ in the world and to follow his teachings through acts of
> compassion, justice, worship, and devotion under the guidance of the Holy Spirit."**

Covenant Discipleship groups write a covenant that spells out how they will follow the teachings of Jesus Christ in their daily lives, shaped by the General Rule. The group's covenant serves as the agenda for the weekly one-hour meeting.

Covenant Discipleship Groups Are . . .

- up to seven persons who meet for one hour each week
- guided by a covenant they write, shaped by the General Rule of Discipleship
- where Christians give a weekly account of how they have witnessed to Jesus Christ in the world and followed his teachings, guided by the group's covenant.
- where Christians help one another become more dependable disciples of Jesus Christ.
- a proven and effective way of nurturing and identifying leaders in discipleship the church needs to live out its mission with Christ in the world.

To Learn More . . .

visit the web site at http://www.umcdiscipleship.org/covenantdiscipleship

Contact: Director of Adult Discipleship
PO Box 340003
Nashville, TN 37203-0003
Email: cdgroups@umcdiscipleship.org
Telephone: (877) 899-2780, ext. 7020 (toll free)

Recommended Resources

Accountable Discipleship: Living in God's Household by Steven W. Manskar
(ISBN: 978-0-88177-339-2)
> Provides Biblical, theological & historic foundations for Covenant Discipleship.

Disciples Making Disciples: Guide for Covenant Discipleship Groups and Class Leaders by Steven W. Manskar (ISBN: 978-0-88177-774-1)
> Essential resource for congregational leaders and Covenant Discipleship group members. Provides valuable information on how to form groups, how to write a covenant, and how to lead a meeting,

Everyday Disciples: Covenant Discipleship with Youth by Chris Wilterdink (ISBN: 978-0-88177-793-2)
> This book is for pastors and youth workers. It provides ideas for youth ministry that effectively helps middle school, senior high, and college students grow in holiness of heart and life.

Growing Everyday Disciples: Covenant Discipleship with Children by Melanie Gordon, Susan Groseclose, and Gayle Quay (ISBN: 978-0-88177-695-9)
> This book is a resource for pastors and leaders responsible for the Christian formation of elementary school age children. It is excellent preparation for confirmation.

Forming Christian Disciples: The Role of Covenant Discipleship and Class Leaders in the Congregation by David Lowes Watson (ISBN: 978-1579109462)
> This is an essential resource for pastors. Watson provides the historic, Biblical, and theological rationale for Covenant Discipleship groups and Class Leaders. He helps the pastor understand their role in the congregation's disciple-making mission.

Help us to help each other, Lord,
Each other's cross to bear;
Let all their friendly aid afford,
And feel each other's care.

Touched by the lodestone of thy love,
Let all our hearts agree,
And ever toward each other move,
And ever move toward thee.

CHARLES WESLEY

Put your Covenant Discipleship group covenant here.

Notes

Notes

Notes

Notes

Notes

Notes

Notes

Notes

CPSIA information can be obtained
at www.ICGtesting.com
Printed in the USA
FFHW011810240819
54431554-60113FF

9 780881 779141